T0328786

Cambridge Elements ☰

Elements in Contentious Politics
edited by
David S. Meyer
University of California, Irvine
and
Suzanne Staggenborg
University of Pittsburgh

THE STREET AND THE BALLOT BOX

Interactions Between Social Movements and Electoral Politics in Authoritarian Contexts

Lynette H. Ong
University of Toronto

CAMBRIDGE
UNIVERSITY PRESS

CAMBRIDGE
UNIVERSITY PRESS

University Printing House, Cambridge CB2 8BS, United Kingdom

One Liberty Plaza, 20th Floor, New York, NY 10006, USA

477 Williamstown Road, Port Melbourne, VIC 3207, Australia

314–321, 3rd Floor, Plot 3, Splendor Forum, Jasola District Centre, New Delhi – 110025, India

103 Penang Road, #05–06/07, Visioncrest Commercial, Singapore 238467

Cambridge University Press is part of the University of Cambridge.

It furthers the University's mission by disseminating knowledge in the pursuit of education, learning, and research at the highest international levels of excellence.

www.cambridge.org
Information on this title: www.cambridge.org/9781009158305
DOI: 10.1017/9781009158268

© Lynette H. Ong 2022

First published 2022

A catalogue record for this publication is available from the British Library.

ISBN 978-1-009-15830-5 Paperback
ISSN 2633-3570 (online)
ISSN 2633-3562 (print)

The Street and the Ballot Box

Interactions Between Social Movements and Electoral Politics in Authoritarian Contexts

Elements in Contentious Politics

DOI: 10.1017/9781009158268
First published online: January 2022

Lynette H. Ong
University of Toronto

Author for correspondence: Lynette H. Ong, Lynette.Ong@utoronto.ca

Abstract: How do discontented masses and opposition elites work together to engineer a change in electoral authoritarian regimes? Social movements and elections are often seen as operating in different terrains – outside and inside institutions, respectively. In this Element, I develop a theory to describe how a broad-based social movement that champions a grievance shared by a wide segment of the population can build alliances across society and opposition elites that, despite the rules of the game rigged against them, vote the incumbents out of power. The broad-based nature of the movement also contributes to the cohesion of the opposition alliance, and elite defection, which are often crucial for regime change. This Element examines the 2018 Malaysian election and draws on a range of cases from other authoritarian regimes across Asia, Eastern Europe, and Africa to illustrate these arguments.

Keywords: social movement, election, autocracy, movement-election interaction, competitive authoritarian, Malaysia.

ISBNs: 9781009158305 (PB), 9781009158268 (OC)
ISSNs: 2633-3570 (online), 2633-3562 (print)

Contents

1 Introduction

1.1 The Much-neglected Interactions Between the Street and the Ballot Box

Social movements and electoral politics are often seen as operating in *different* terrains: the former in the extra-institutional arena, and the latter within an institutional framework. Despite the growth in literature since the 1990s examining their interactions, social movement activists are still primarily considered outsiders to political processes. As Charles Tilly has observed, social movements are seen as "challengers" seeking to enter the institutionalized work of "polity members," who have routinized access to the levers of power (Tilly, 1978). However, to shape electoral outcomes, movements and parties often straddle in between institutional and extra-institutional arenas. Grievances drive movements, and movement activists strategize to influence the behavior of institutional actors and change institutional outcomes.

To observers of social movements, institutionalization is often associated with demobilization, in that once movement activists pursue institutionalized channels, mobilization actions are expected to fade away. Central to this view is the perception that protest is for outsiders and opponents of the institutional system, while those within the system pursue institutional means such as lobbying, voting, and the legal system to realize their objectives. However, in reality, there is only a fuzzy – and often times permeable – boundary between institutionalized and noninstitutionalized politics (Goldstone, 2003, pp. 1–26).

Social movements and elections are thus more interactive than most scholars have assumed. As McAdam & Tarrow (2010) argue, "social movements and elections are not discrete and separate events, but mutually constitutive forms of politics that often interact to shape the prospects for both short and longer term social and political change." Movements produce collective actions that influence elections; join electoral coalitions and turn into political parties; engage in proactive electoral mobilization; engage in reactive electoral mobilization; polarize political parties internally; and mobilize or demobilize in response to shifts in electoral regimes (McAdam & Tarrow, 2010, p. 553). It is therefore pertinent to examine causal effects of social movements on electoral politics and the interactions between them, because when *studied in isolation*, some crucial relationships might be missed.

1.2 What Is the Puzzle?

Opposition parties in competitive authoritarian regimes, or illiberal regimes in general, face an uphill battle in defeating the authoritarian incumbents.

Electoral rules and institutions are often controlled and manipulated by the autocrats to preclude fair competition (Diamond, 2002; Levitsky & Way, 2002). Incumbents tilt the playing field by buying votes (Blaydes, 2010; Lust-Okar, 2006), coopting elites and societal groups (Boix & Svolik, 2007; Magaloni, 2006), controlling media resources, and gerrymandering electoral districts to give greater representation to supporters (Lust-Okar, 2005; Malesky, 2009). When institutional channels prevent the opposition from competing fairly or winning an election, what are the noninstitutional resources and routes available to effectuate regime change?

Most studies on movement–election interactions have focused on democratic contexts, while authoritarian contexts have largely been overlooked. Accordingly, this Element analyzes the dynamics of pre- and postelection movements, respectively, to understand how they contribute to liberalizing political outcomes in authoritarian regimes. The first section examines why fraudulent elections give rise to mass mobilization, and under what conditions postelection mobilization brings about successful revolutionary outcomes. The second section investigates how a broad-based movement can build an effective opposition coalition, and under what circumstances it will become a competitive electoral contender that eventually defeats the authoritarian incumbents.

By parsing the causal mechanisms through which "stolen elections" lead to mass uprisings and the toppling of autocratic rulers, I argue that movement–election interactions are critical to understanding regime change in authoritarian contexts. A fraudulent election is a political opportunity that produces powerful emotions of moral outrage that spurs people to take to the streets, and changes their cost–benefit calculation of protest participation in high-risk authoritarian settings. Once it reaches a critical scale, mass uprisings may change the elites' calculations, prompting some close allies of the rulers to defect, which in turn precipitates regime downfall. I survey a range of country cases across Eastern Europe and Southeast Asia to analyze how different conditions produce successful and unsuccessful revolutionary outcomes. These conditions include widespread regime grievances, availability of mobilizing structures, the movement's critical mass, strategic choice of violent versus nonviolent resistance, elite defection, and Western intervention.

Next, I develop a new theory to explicate how a broad-based movement can contribute to building a coherent opposition coalition capable of defeating the electoral incumbents. The theory underscores two factors necessary to bring about regime change: a strong opposition coalition rooted in a broad-based social movement that mobilizes across social cleavages, and the credibility and cohesiveness of the opposition alliance. Political opportunities that spike antiregime sentiments and cause elite defection, such as economic crises and major corruption scandals, can be very helpful in producing a regime-changing outcome.

Using process tracing of sociopolitical changes in Malaysia over two decades (1998–2018), this study inductively builds a theory that explains the causal mechanisms through which a broad-based social movement leads to regime change. Namely, broad-based social movements facilitate the formation of an effective opposition coalition, creating the preconditions for regime change. The theory stresses the necessity of a broad-based movement *before* electoral competition due to its crucial role in bringing together all antiregime forces. It departs from the existing literature on authoritarianism by accentuating mass mobilization that takes place prior to – rather than after – the elections. In other words, a movement per se does not topple autocratic rulers; it helps to forge unity among antiregime forces, and build an opposition coalition strong and competitive enough to bring down autocratic rulers. This amounts to the appropriation of extra-institutional societal strength (through a broad-based movement) to effectuate a liberalizing institutional outcome (of regime change) when the institution (of opposition parties) is not strong enough. The reciprocal processes between institutions and extra-institutions can be long and arduous, as the case of Malaysia amply illustrates. Yet, they may be necessary to bring about regime change in divided societies or plurality electoral systems where the electoral opposition faces strong hurdles in cross-mobilization and defeating the incumbents.

1.3 Theoretical Contributions

1.3.1 Interactions Between Social Movements and Electoral Politics in Democracies and Non-democracies

The existing literature on movement–election interactions has largely centered on Western democracies. Within this context, the literature finds that modern political parties are the outgrowth of social movements (Goldstone, 2003, pp. 1–26; Kubik, 1998). In addition, movements can transform into movement parties, such as the Western European green parties in the 1970s and 1980s, which were more likely to arise in proportional representation systems (Kitschelt & Hellemans, 1990; Kitschelt, 1989) than in two-party majoritarian systems like that of the US (Kriesi *et al.*, 1995). Tarrow (2021) finds that movements and political parties in the US have continuously influenced one another from the Civil War to the contemporary period.

Long-established mainstream political parties have had to co-opt social movements and rely on movements' grassroots support to win elections

(Dalton & Kuechler, 1990; Kriesi *et al.*, 1995). This has led to the emergence of a "movement society" that blurs the distinction between contentious and conventional politics, and between institutional and noninstitutional politics (Meyer & Tarrow, 1998, p. 25). As well, the two major parties in the US have veered away from the "median voter" in order to court those at the margins of the ideological and policy spectrums, particularly those on the far right (McAdam & Kloos, 2014). This has caused partisan polarization (Heaney & Rojas, 2015; Schlozman, 2015), manifested in the 2010s Tea Party movement (Skocpol & Williamson, 2016), as well as in Trumpism and the anti-Trump movement (Meyer & Tarrow, 2018). Increased polarization has profound implications for electoral representation in that the "median voter" convergence theory may give way to democratic backsliding (Svolik, 2019).

Meanwhile, relatively little work has been done on how movements and electoral politics interact to shape regime outcomes in authoritarian contexts, with the exception of post-"stolen election" mobilization. In electoral autocracies, fraudulent elections often provide the impetus for postelection mass uprisings by creating public discontent, moral outrage, and changing the cost–benefit calculation of protest participation (Tucker, 2007; Kuntz & Thompson, 2009). Mass demonstrations make the incumbents look weak, and cause some ruling elites to defect and join the opposition. Postelection mass movements further serve to unite antiregime forces, and foster collaboration between civil society and the opposition (Bunce & Wolchik, 2010; Trejo, 2014). Successful democratic revolutions in neighboring states that provide positive illustrative examples can lead to modular revolutions (Beissinger, 2007). Figure 1.1 is a schematic representation of how social movements and elite coalitions interact to shape regime outcomes.

This study contributes to the literature on authoritarianism and movement–election interactions by illustrating how a preelection broad-based movement helps to forge opposition–civil society collaboration and overcome social fragmentation. The nature of a broad-based movement is one that advances a grievance widely shared across society, and is identifiable by elites and nonelites alike. In resource mobilization theory, NGOs and other mobilizing structures serve to mobilize members into collective actions. However, when a broad-based movement becomes a means, rather than an end, it does *not* only mobilize discontented masses into collective actions; more importantly, the movement forges an informal partnership between opposition elites and the masses, helping them to build an effective opposition coalition capable of defeating the incumbents.

The pertinence of opposition coalitions goes beyond the coordination problem that the existing literature has examined at length (Bunce & Wolchik, 2011; Donno, 2013; Howard & Roessler, 2006). Besides solving the coordination problem, this study underscores the fact that a cohesive opposition coalition also *sustains* the alliance after it has won power. It also argues for the importance of a credible opposition alliance, one that is able to convince the voters of its capacity to govern once it wins power. Credibility and cohesion, which serve distinct purposes, can be hard to reach for opposition groups competing against long-term autocrats. Incumbent autocrats are armed with resources to divide dissenting voices, and their monopolization of political power precludes opponents from gaining governing experience.

"Stolen elections" serve as a political opportunity (Meyer, 2004; Meyer & Staggenborg, 1996) for civil society and opposition groups in electoral autocracies to mobilize collective actions. Owing to international pressure or desire to maintain procedural legitimacy, autocrats may promise to hold elections. But, when elections are rigged, the masses may become outraged and turn out in hordes to protest. Mass demonstrations cause antiregime sentiments to spike, shake the foundations of autocratic regimes, and encourage elite defection that precipitates regime downfall. This study illustrates that a preelection mass movement can *similarly* benefit from a political opportunity that spurs antiregime sentiments and leads to elite defection. Together, these forces contribute to building an effective opposition coalition capable of bringing about regime change.

1.3.2 Democratization Literature: Shining the Spotlight on Movements and Civil Society

Democratization is a vast but fragmented field of study. While it is beyond the scope here to provide an extensive review, in this section, I will highlight how this study on movement–election interactions contributes to the democratization literature. Democratization is usually seen as a function of either socioeconomic preconditions, such as level of economic development and income inequality, or elite behavior (Geddes, 1999; Haggard & Kaufman, 2016b). Meanwhile, nonelite actors are typically considered marginal in democratization studies (della Porta, 2014), whereas social movements are seen as a symptom rather than a cause of democratizing outcomes (Collier, 1999; Linz & Stepan, 1996). In Guillermo O'Donnell and Philippe Schmitter's own words, "regardless of its intensity and of the background from which it emerges, this popular upsurge is always *ephemeral*" (O'Donnell *et al.*, 1986, pp. 55–56; italics added)

There are, however, some notable exceptions. Studies on the role of civil society in democratization have traditionally focused on unions' capacity to mobilize collective action for political change (Collier, 1999; Rueschemeyer *et al.*, 1992). More recently, mass mobilization has been seen as an important factor in democratic transition (Haggard & Kaufman, 2012, 2016a), as have social media networks (Tufekci & Wilson, 2012). Social movements are also vital in the democratic consolidation phase as they keep elites under popular pressure, though democratic transitions can demobilize civil society organizations and transform them into institutional actors (Karatnycky & Ackerman, 2005).

1.3.3 What Causes Democratization? Contentious Politics versus Elite Pacts

To assess the impact of popular actions on political authorities, social movement scholars have focused on contentious collective actions (Tarrow, 1989, 1998; Tilly, 1978) that are intended to subvert or challenge authorities (Beissinger, 2002). It, however, begs the questions of whether contentious actions make a difference to political outcome on their own or by influencing the strategic choices of elites. The "moderation argument" argues that too much popular mobilization or bottom-up pressure reduces the likelihood of democratization (Bermeo, 1997). The concern is that if mass actors gained control over traditional ruling classes, it would destabilize the regime transition (Karl, 1990). The "threat from below" must therefore be moderated, so the argument goes (Kaufman, 1986, p. 88). However, the fear of the mob may be overstated: "in many cases, democratization seems to have proceeded alongside weighty and even bloody popular challenges" (Bermeo, 1997, p. 314). Social movement scholars make a stronger claim that popular contention forges cross-class coalitions and co-opts excluded groups that can help with the democratization process (McAdam *et al.*, 2001). The effects of contentious actions on regime outcomes could depend on regime type: single-party and military regimes are more likely to break down following nonviolent protests, but the same cannot be said about personalistic regimes (Ulfelder, 2005).

Dan Slater (2010) argues that violent insurgencies, particularly urban riots, help forge "protection pacts" among political elites as they fear loss of power and privileges from social disorder. Cross-elite coalitions in turn build strong states and contribute to authoritarian durability. Using this reasoning, he explains why the violent contentious politics in Malaysia in 1969 and in Indonesia in 1965 ended up cementing the strength of the ruling parties in the two countries. This argument establishes a direct link between contentious politics and elite pacts by assessing how they combine to influence regime outcomes. Slater (2010) belongs to the social conflict origins genre of scholarship that critiques the institutional turn in the studies of authoritarianism (Pepinsky, 2014). This body of scholarly work treats elite coalitions as institutions that are endogenous to the underlying social relations (see also Brownlee, 2007). Figure 1.1 illustrates how the nature of contentious politics influences elite institutions, which in turn shape regime outcomes.

Along a similar logic, this study attributes the nature of political coalitions to the underlying social conflicts, or lack thereof. Taking regime change as an outcome (the converse of "regime durability" in studies of authoritarianism), this study centers on the coalition among opposition – rather than ruling – elites as the institution, the strength of which is explained by the preceding nonviolent broad-based social movement as illustrated in Figure 1.1. Existing literature explains how violent social conflicts bring political elites together out of fear of being usurped by radical social forces, which serves to strengthen authoritarian regimes. This Element advances a diametrical logic to explain authoritarian breakdown – that is, nonviolent mass mobilization that rallies discontented groups across society helps to build strong opposition coalitions, which destabilizes authoritarian regimes. This line of reasoning applies to post-stolen-election mass mobilization as well as preelection social movements, both of which contribute to regime-changing outcomes.

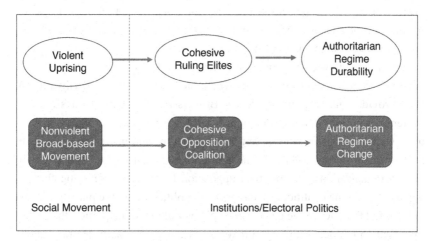

Figure 1.1 How contentious politics interact with elite coalitions to shape regime outcomes.

Source: Author's illustration.

1.3.4 Social Movement Literature: Nonviolent Resistance; Brokerage Between Movement and Party; Movement-rooted Political Coalition

Social movement studies typically treat movements as an outcome, analyzing different conditions, opportunities, and mechanisms that make them successful or otherwise. By contrast, the present study frames social movements as a *means* to an end, rather than an end in itself. In other words, a broad-based movement is a stepping stone to the formation of an elite opposition coalition, which is the actual agency that brings about the regime-changing outcome.

Studies on the broad-based movement in Malaysia uphold the efficacy of nonviolent civil resistance, as Chenoweth and Stephan (2011) and Schock (2015) have argued. However, it is not because a nonviolent movement per se is more likely to topple an authoritarian regime. Rather, nonviolent movements are more capable of rallying and accommodating various antiregime forces on a common platform by lowering the high cost of protest participation in an authoritarian context.

More importantly, the creation of a broad-based movement that coalesces cross-sectional antiregime elements, and its subsequent transformation into an institutional coalition, is brokered by a group of political entrepreneurs who have one foot in party politics, and another foot in civil society activism. These political entrepreneurs exercise the function of brokerage, which is a relational mechanism in social contention that "links two or more currently unconnected social sites by a unit that mediates their relations with each other and/or with yet another site" (McAdam *et al.*, 2001, p. 142). These brokers are called "movement-partisans" in US politics, per Heaney and Rojas (2007)'s term, who create reciprocal processes between movements and parties, and sustain party–movement alliances (Schlozman, 2015).

Yet, the broad-based movement in Malaysia underscores the salient role of brokers beyond social contention, for which McAdam, Tarrow, and Tilly (2001) have provided authoritative evidence. Brokers are also key in transforming contentious politics into electoral opposition coalitions, as Section 3 will illustrate. Opposition elites who broker between parties and movements establish a platform to accommodate disenchanted masses from across society, civil society organizations, and political opposition figures who come together as a grand antiregime coalition. In authoritarian polities where the playing field is unlevel and the rules of the game rigged in favor of the ruling parties, the cross-mobilization of society through brokerage of movement–party interactions is a creative strategy by the opposition to address structural disadvantages in electoral competition.

When a movement is treated as a means to a political end, we can trace the strength of the opposition coalition to the preceding social movement in which it is rooted (LeBas, 2011). This study further illustrates that a broad-based movement with strong roots penetrating into society, combined with collaboration between opposition parties and civil society, is more likely to create an opposition coalition that qualifies as a serious electoral contender. Mass mobilization with strong breadth and depth is capable of producing a liberalizing political outcome, not through the oftentimes nonviolent revolutionary actions (Beissinger, 2013; della Porta, 2014; Nepstad, 2011), but by building a coherent opposition coalition that can compete with the authoritarian incumbents. In brief, this Element contributes to the social movement literature by catenating it with the cognate and yet unconnected fields of liberalizing electoral outcomes (Howard & Roessler, 2006; Morgenbesser & Pepinsky, 2019; Wahman, 2013), institutional coalition building (Arriola, 2012; Bunce & Wolchik, 2011; Golder, 2006), and democratization.

1.4 Organization of the Element

The rest of this volume is organized as follows. Section 2 examines how "stolen elections" create a political opportunity that mobilizes people to produce revolutionary change. Drawing upon a range of country cases from Eastern Europe and Asia, the section analyzes the conditions that lead to successful and unsuccessful revolutionary outcomes. While Section 2 focuses on mass mobilization after elections, the following section proposes a theory and a set of causal mechanisms that explicates how a broad-based social movement can absorb and amass antiregime forces to facilitate the formation of an opposition alliance and eventually bring about regime change.

The theory advanced in Section 3 is inductively derived from tracing the empirical details of movement rallies and electoral outcomes over a twenty-year period in Malaysia, from the Reformasi movement in 1998 to the first Bersih rally in 2007, and the four subsequent rallies that eventually led to the toppling of the authoritarian incumbents at the historic 2018 election. I illustrate how and why the first few rally–election interactions failed to defeat the incumbents, despite the presence of various opposition coalitions facilitated by movements. At each subsequent round of movement-opposition alliance building, however, the incumbents saw their advantages gradually chipped away. The massive sovereign wealth fund corruption scandal that implicated the former prime minister presented a political opportunity that significantly inflamed antiregime sentiments. A new broad-based electoral movement, Bersih, capitalized on the opportunity by uniting all antiregime forces, including former regime insiders, under its banner. It also facilitated the formation of an opposition coalition that was credible and cohesive enough to win the next election and end the sixty-one-year rule of the National Front alliance.[1]

The logic of street politics *preceding* institutional politics underscores the difference a movement with a widely shared grievance can make at the ballot box, as the case of Malaysia demonstrates. Institutional actors in autocratic regimes are bound by the rules of the game, which are often rigged against them if they are part of the opposition. When electoral change proves to be extremely challenging, street politics can coalesce, unite, and build the institutional strength necessary to defeat the incumbents.

2 From Stolen Election to Mass Mobilization and Regime Change

The existing literature on movement–election interactions in authoritarian contexts focuses predominantly on mass mobilization that follows rigged or "stolen" elections, which, on some occasions, leads to regime change. In authoritarian regimes, the incumbents are able to manipulate electoral institutions, resulting in an uneven playing field for the opposition parties. This still begs the question of why some mass mobilization movements succeed in bringing down the regime whereas others do not. This is the central inquiry in this section.

Autocratic governments may hold regular elections, but they often employ unfair tactics, such as gerrymandering, monopolization of campaign finances, control of the media, and vote rigging, to tilt the playing field in their favor. Using coercive strategies, these governments can keep the opposition divided, and permanently weaken their electoral opponents. Despite these advantages, an election that is overtly rigged by the incumbents risks inviting a backlash in the form of mass mobilization. When fraudulent elections give rise to popular discontent, postelection mass mobilization serves to convey to domestic and international audiences the autocratic nature of the regime, and its weakness or vulnerability (Schedler, 2013, p. 301).

Stolen elections can lead to mass mobilization through two means: they can be seen as a political opportunity that stokes antiregime grievances and moral outrage that spurs people to go out onto the street, or they can change people's rational cost–benefit calculation of participating in collective action. The stolen election–mass mobilization interactions can lead to regime change by providing an organizational strategy for mobilizing across elite and societal groups. This

---

[1] Section Three builds on an earlier paper, "From Voice to Vote: Electoral Movement, Coalitional Politics, and Regime Change in Malaysia" (January 14, 2019). Available at https://papers .ssrn.com/sol3/papers.cfm?abstract_id=3868285.

increases the success rates of revolutions and can provide a modular process of emulation, which facilitates revolutionary changes in neighboring countries.

Postelection mass uprisings, however, do not always lead to regime change. This section draws upon cases from the "Color Revolutions" in Eastern Europe and autocracies in Asia to analyze the conditions that give rise to revolutionary success. The important conditions for determining success are nonviolent resistance that lowers the costs of participation, and the availability of civil society organizations to serve as mobilizing structures to rally people across society, both of which contribute to forming a critical mass of protestors. Once a "threshold" in size is reached, autocratic regimes start to look weak, which tends to instigate elite defection and precipitate regime downfall.

2.1 Mechanisms of Stolen Election Mobilization–Regime Change Interaction

As illustrated in Figure 2.1, the causality from stolen elections to regime change involves two sets of mechanisms: one that leads from stolen elections to mass mobilization (A), and the other that leads from mass mobilization to regime change (B). This first set of interactions shows mass mobilization triggered by fraudulent or "stolen" elections – when autocratic governments rig electoral results to declare victory. The second set of interactions reflects popular discontent giving rise to mass uprisings, with some autocrats forced to hand over power, and others managing to stay on.

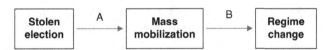

Figure 2.1 From stolen elections to mass mobilization and regime change.

2.1.1 From Stolen Election to Mass Mobilization

Stolen elections can provide a focal point for the mobilization of large-scale collective actions in a number of ways. As relatively infrequent but scheduled events, elections tend to attract widespread international attention. When they are stolen, they can produce powerful emotions of moral outrage, which spur people to engage in street protests. Emotions may be particularly important in driving the first few hundred people to go out onto the street (Kuran, 1991). Stolen elections also create the collective frame of being "cheated" by the regime, which helps to coalesce a large segment of the population around a common grievance (Kuntz & Thompson, 2009).

However, while stolen elections often provoke moral outrage, citizens may not necessarily go out to the street because contentious actions in autocratic settings are likely to invite reprisal. Thus, citizens who face high costs for participating in collective actions may falsify their public preferences (Kuran, 1991). However, once a sufficiently large number of people congregate, it can change people's rational cost–benefit calculation of protest participation (Tucker, 2007). Shared grievances around stolen elections can also address the collective action problem by lowering the risks of being punished because participants become one of the many who stand up against autocratic regimes (Tucker, 2007).

2.1.2 From Stolen Election-Mass Mobilization to Regime Change

Stolen elections provide antiregime forces with the political opportunity to mobilize across elite and societal groups. Mass uprisings change the calculation of elites, including the military and the ruler's close allies. As they witness the emergence of a new power center backed by the people, they may decide to abandon the leadership. Besides elites, postelection movements help to overcome opposition disunity and foster collaboration among the political opposition, civil society groups, and foreign governments (Bunce & Wolchik, 2010, pp. 50–51). Given the significance of a unified opposition in defeating an incumbent in electoral autocracies, the mobilizing capacity of postelection movements improves the likelihood of regime change.

Civil society is another important factor in mobilizing the opposition. It plays a crucial role in mobilizing voters to go to the polls, monitoring elections, overseeing electoral procedures, and denouncing fraud in stolen elections. By exposing how the autocrats had rigged the elections, civil society helped to garner support from the masses and overthrow the autocratic regimes in the "Color Revolutions" (Bunce & Wolchik, 2010, pp. 71–73; Trejo, 2014, p. 335).

Since participating in a revolution involves high risks, successful democratic revolutions in neighboring states provide positive transnational proof of success, which bolsters people's confidence in joining street protests. Modular revolutions such as these contributed to successes throughout the former Soviet bloc in the 2000s, including the "Bulldozer Revolution" in Serbia, the "Orange Revolution" in Ukraine, the "Rose Revolution" in Georgia, and the "Tulip Revolution" in Kyrgyzstan (Beissinger, 2007).

2.2 Theoretical Discussion

What is the role of stolen elections in bringing about regime change? A stolen election is a *political opportunity* (Meyer, 2004; Meyer & Staggenborg, 1996), in social movement parlance, that helps to bring together larger population segments than is possible under normal conditions. Due to external pressures or the need to maintain procedural legitimacy internally, autocrats often hold elections – but cheat in them. Fraudulent elections provide windows of opportunities to expose or increase the vulnerabilities of autocratic regimes to potential mass uprisings. Because elections are important political events that attract international attention, they raise the costs of repression for autocratic regimes, and expand the opportunities for popular protests accordingly (Bunce & Wolchik, 2011, pp. 10–16).

Other political opportunities include economic crises that create profound economic grievances (Brancati, 2016), succession crises that result in leadership vacuums (Hale, 2006), assassinations of widely revered opposition figures that trigger public outrage (Jasper, 1997), or shifts in international alliances that weaken the regime domestically (Bunce, 1999). The Philippines, for example, was in severe economic trouble on the eve of the People Power movement because of plundering by the Marcos family. The assassination of Benigno Aquino Jr., a widely revered leader, created moral outrage that further mobilized support for antiregime mass mobilization in the Philippines. In China, the death of Hu Yaobang, a respected liberal reformist leader, was the lightning rod to the Tiananmen protests in 1989.

It should be underscored that stolen elections per se do not cause regime changes; it is postelection mass protests with support from large swaths of the population that effectively topple authoritarian regimes. Mass mobilization shores up the power of the people and the opposition, and simultaneously makes the autocrats look weak. Put simply, in the case of *postelection* mass mobilization, massive uprisings provide the agency that brings about regime change, whereas stolen elections give the impetus (or political opportunity) to the agency to act. As a prelude, the next section contrasts this argument by examining *preelection* mass mobilization, which has similarly benefitted from a political opportunity (of a corruption scandal), to result in a regime change.

What are the conditions for mass mobilization to successfully bring about regime change? The seven conditions below are generic to all mass mobilizations – and can be used equally to explain the success or otherwise of postelection mobilization. The first two conditions describe the role of stolen elections as a political event that fuels antiregime sentiments and spurs contentious actions. The third and fourth conditions address the organizational platforms and the critical mass necessary to bring about successful revolutionary outcomes. The fifth condition highlights the saliency of nonviolent resistance in bringing about revolutionary outcomes, and establishes linkages with elite defection, the sixth condition. The seventh and last condition addresses the role of international intervention.

First, widespread antiregime grievances exist that hurt the regime's legitimacy: stolen elections often create moral outrage across society that galvanizes people to take part in mass demonstrations. Amid popular disenchantment, fraudulent elections serve as focal points around which aggrieved citizens organize collective actions. Other events, such as economic crises, deaths of revered leaders, and corruption scandals implicating the ruling elites, can similarly create intense antiregime grievances and stimulate revolts.

Second, antiregime sentiments must be overwhelming to drive people to act on their own beliefs or to end preference falsification (Kuran, 1991), either out of moral indignation or based on a rational cost–benefit calculation. Overwhelming popular disenchantment is required in authoritarian contexts due to the inherent high costs of participating in revolutionary actions, given the risk of state reprisal (Davenport, 2007).

Third, mobilizing structures to organize and coordinate citizens' collective actions need to be available (McAdam, 1982; Tarrow, 1998). Authoritarian governments tend to control civil society organizations that could serve as mobilizing structures, such as labor unions, religious organizations, and student bodies, through channeling and other repressive strategies (Earl, 2011). To the extent that domestic NGOs are hamstrung by autocratic states, foreign civil society organizations, such as the National Endowment for Democracy and Open Society Foundation, can play a crucial role in facilitating cross-national training for movement activists.

Fourth, a critical mass is needed to bring down autocratic regimes. The protest size in the successful cases of Serbia and Ukraine, as part of the "Color Revolutions," was between 500,000 and a million, compared to the unsuccessful case of Belarus, which only had 20,000 people at its peak (Franklin, 2019).[2] Mass protests organized by civil society organizations capable of mobilizing large numbers of people across society are key to bringing about revolutionary change.

Fifth, the strategic choice of nonviolent resistance has been recognized as an effective strategy (Chenoweth & Stephan, 2011; Roberts *et al.*, 1967; Schock, 2015), despite the often nondichotomous violent versus nonviolent nature of contentious actions (Case, 2020). Among the nonviolent resistance techniques, defections of the military or police that erode the state's coercive capacity was the most critical (Chenoweth & Stephan, 2011; Nepstad, 2011). For instance, the protestors in Ukraine's "Orange Revolution" held a series of meetings with the army and secret service to persuade them not to use force against civilians, which led to the military leaders' abstention from violence (Binnendijk & Marovic, 2006).

---

[2] Franklin suggests maximum, not median, protest sizes are positively correlated with revolutionary success.

Similarly, the defection of two high-profile military leaders in the Philippines publicized a fissure in the armed forces, which encouraged low-ranking security officers to defect. Once army officers deserted the regime en masse, Marcos's autocratic state lost its capacity to repress contentious activities (Nepstad, 2011, p. 129; Romulo, 1987, pp. 230–231).

Sixth, revolutionary outcomes are more likely to be realized in the case of elite defection, and ruling elites who switch their allegiance can bring with them groups of supporters when they join the opposition. Regimes are unlikely to be toppled if they enjoy unified support from ruling elites (Bunce & Wolchik, 2011; Goldstone, 2001; Nepstad, 2011). These elites are those in the ruler's inner circle, military leaders, wealthy oligarchs who provide financial support, and key personnel in the coercive apparatus.

Seventh, Western intervention, or lack thereof, is also a relevant condition. All the successful modular "Color Revolutions" benefited from funding and activist training provided or facilitated by the US government and other organizations, namely the National Endowment of Democracy (NED) and George Soros's Open Society Foundations. In the unsuccessful cases, Russia's capacity to influence domestic politics, and lack of US intervention due to strategic considerations appear to be relevant factors in explaining why mass protests did not bring about regime change. Countries with high Western linkages or intense economic, social, or political ties, and over which Western countries have leverage are more likely to face consistent and effective democratizing pressure (Levitsky & Way, 2006).

2.3 Successful and Unsuccessful Cases of Revolutionary Change

This section provides a range of country cases of mass uprisings, some of which resulted in successful regime change, while others did not. These cases are selected to provide variations in the conditions described earlier and to assess their contribution to the outcome variable of revolutionary change.

In the successful cases of Serbia, Ukraine, and Georgia that were all part of the "Color Revolutions," and the Philippines, nonviolent resistance organized by civil society organizations that reached a critical mass were common essential conditions. Military and other security leaders' defection or abstention from using violence against protestors was also an important factor. However, elite defection did not come from a vacuum; it was often a result of mass uprisings that significantly weakened the autocratic regimes. In the failed cases of Azerbaijan and Belarus, a combination of factors, such as violent crackdowns, lack of unity among the opposition, and constrained civil society, meant that demonstrations did not reach a critical mass and the autocratic regimes were able to hold on to power.

2.3.1 "Bulldozer Revolution" in Serbia

Serbia under Slobodan Milošević was a competitive authoritarian regime that engaged in ethnic cleansing, as well as the harassment of opposition, media, and civil society organizations, though he never outlawed them. Milošević's clever strategies of labeling himself as a nationalist, scapegoating minority populations, and "playing up threats" of disintegration had kept him in power (Bunce & Wolchik, 2011, p. 92). Divided by ideology and personalities, the opposition elites were not popular among the people (Bunce & Wolchik, 2011, pp. 95–96). However, the formation of two civil society organizations in the 1990s, the Center for Elections and Democracy (CeSID) and the student movement Otpor, began to pose a challenge to the regime (Bunce & Wolchik, 2011, p. 97).

Milošević called an election in 2000 that he did not view as a threat to his power, but it presented democratic activists and foreign democracy promoters with a political opportunity to unseat him. With funding from international donors, CeSID and Otpor mobilized voters and workers to convince ordinary Serbians that regime change was possible (Bunce & Wolchik, 2011, p. 107).[3] Serbia's opposition parties agreed to put aside their differences to create a united opposition coalition (McFaul, 2005, p. 10). These efforts paid off as the people turned out in hordes on voting day, but the opposition watched in dismay when Milošević declared a victory. Following the fraudulent election, the opposition called for a general strike, and was joined by coal miners who supplied 70 percent of the country's energy (Bunce & Wolchik, 2011, p. 110). This led to elite defection, including among military leaders. An estimated 500,000 to a million Serbians marched peacefully in Belgrade, in what is known as the "Bulldozer Revolution," which eventually forced Milošević to hand over power (Bunce & Wolchik, 2011, pp. 110–111).

2.3.2 "Orange Revolution" in Ukraine

The 2004 presidential election in Ukraine was held in a highly charged political atmosphere, with allegations of media bias, voter intimidation, and the poisoning of opposition candidates. Civil society organizations mobilized voter turnout and organized information campaigns to topple the incumbent leader, Viktor Yanukovych (Bunce & Wolchik, 2011, pp. 133–136). When Yanukovych was declared the winner, the opposition parties and NGOs worked together to mobilize people for postelection protests, building on their prior collaborative relationship (Bunce & Wolchik, 2011, pp. 135–137). This resulted in widespread peaceful demonstrations, dubbed the "Orange Revolution" (McFaul, 2005). The

---

[3] The US government, and various US foundations, committed as much as $41 million to promoting democratic change in Serbia through youth organizations, such as Otpor. See Beissinger (2007).

mass uprising also helped to forge unity among economic elites, namely the wealthy oligarchs, and defectors from the president's inner circle.

On the day the regime declared a fraudulent "victory," the civil society organizations Pora and "Our Ukraine," helped by small business owners and the Kyiv city government, set up hundreds of tents near Independence Square in Kyiv to keep protestors fed, clean, and warm (McFaul, 2005, p. 14). The military and the police had decided to stay neutral by not blocking people's transport access and refusing to use violence against protestors (Bunce & Wolchik, 2011, pp. 139–140). This was part of the protestors' nonviolent strategy, as they engaged in dialogues with the military to dissuade them from deploying violence. Once the protest size reached a critical mass, the costs of violent repression became significantly higher for the regime, which eventually forced Yanukovych to hand over power to Victor Yushchenko (Bunce & Wolchik, 2011, p. 140).[4]

2.3.3 "Rose Revolution" in Georgia

The "Rose Revolution" that toppled President Eduard Shevardnadze in 2003 came after a rigged parliamentary election. The opposition in Georgia had taken advantage of the regime's weakness on the eve of the election, but did not collaborate with civil society to the extent its counterparts in Serbia or Ukraine did, and postelection protests were of a relatively smaller scale (Bunce & Wolchik, 2011, p. 164). Since the late 1980s, Moscow had experienced a sharp decline in its ability to influence politics in the Soviet bloc, which gave rise to nationalist movement in Georgia (Bunce & Wolchik, 2011, pp. 150–151). In the late 1990s, Georgia's economic recovery was affected by Russia's economic crisis, which became "a turning point" for Shevardnadze's regime (Bunce & Wolchik, 2011, p. 154). Popular support for Shevardnadze began to plummet amidst growing corruption, fraudulent elections, inadequate public goods provision, and his lack of reform commitment. US support also began to wane due to lack of democratic progress.

Prior to the 2003 election, student-led protests in 2001 had taken the government and opposition by surprise. As the regime's power weakened, Mikheil Saakashvili, the minister of justice, defected to the opposition (Bunce & Wolchik, 2011, p. 156). Civil society had grown rapidly prior to the protests, largely funded by the US government and George Soros's Open Society Foundations. The Georgian youth organization, Kmara, had adopted the

---

[4] By way of contrast, Beissinger (2013) argues that rather than being driven by the desire for democratic change, participants in the Orange Revolution shared cultural practices, language, and religious identities. Identity trumped ideology and grievances, which mobilized those who shared negative sentiments about the regime.

organizational template from its Serbian counterpart, Otpor, and learned about protest and electoral techniques, such as voter registration and mobilization (Bunce & Wolchik, 2011, pp. 160–162; Meladze, 2005). Saakashvili ran an extraordinarily effective campaign in the 2003 parliamentary election that brought him strong political support. Shevardnadze, like Milošević in Serbia, was not interested in campaigning as he had never had to do so to win votes previously (Bunce & Wolchik, 2011, p. 164). Eventually, Shevardnadze was brought down in the "Rose Revolution" by nonviolent mass protests organized by civil society organizations.

Youth movements played an important role in modular revolutions in Serbia, Ukraine, and Georgia. A Georgian youth group visited Belgrade in 2003 on an Open Society Foundations-sponsored trip, during which they learned about the Serbian youth movement, Otpor. Upon returning to Georgia, they founded their own movement, Kmara ("Enough"). From Otpor, Kmara activists learned the techniques of nonviolent resistance and voter mobilization, borrowed its clenched fist logo, and considered the Serbian group "a huge source of inspiration" (Beissinger, 2007, pp. 260–262). Pora, the Ukrainian youth movement that played a crucial role in the "Orange Revolution," was also heavily influenced by Otpor.

2.3.4 "People Power Movement" in the Philippines

The toppling of the regime of Ferdinand Marcos in the Philippines in 1986 following a rigged election and mass uprising, known as the "People Power Movement," offers another example of successful postelection revolutionary change. Under Marcos's personalist rule, the plundering and exploitation of national assets were rampant (Thompson, 1996, p. 182). The legitimacy of Marcos's regime declined as personal plundering mounted, and the circle of cronies narrowed to his family members and close friends (Hutchcroft, 1991, pp. 429–434). Foreign aid and loans ended up in private bank accounts, resulting in stagnant growth and a debt crisis. After years of martial law, Marcos agreed to hold elections in 1978. Though controlled by the government, the ability to compete in elections gave rise to an antiregime coalition, consisting of opposition parties, students, urban movements, professional associations, and Catholic grassroots movements, which were involved in waves of mobilization between 1978 and 1986 (Thompson, 1996).

The assassination of Benigno Aquino, a revered opposition leader, in 1983 angered many Filipinos, and stoked a cross-class civil resistance movement (Thompson, 1995). The Catholic Church played an important role in coalescing the noncommunist opposition and Manila's business elites (Mendoza, 2009). In order to shore up his weak political position, Marcos decided to call a snap election in 1986, presenting antiregime forces with a political opportunity to topple him (Morgenbesser & Pepinsky, 2019). The fraudulent election led to a massive uprising, with millions of Filipinos from all walks of life engaging in nonviolent resistance in metro Manila (Mendoza, 2009; Schock, 2005). These contentious activities were possible because of Marcos's comparatively lesser repression, unlike the ruling parties in neighboring Indonesia and Burma that eliminated all regime opponents (Boudreau, 2004).

A combination of mass protests, external pressure from the US, and continued economic hardships led to elite defection. When the cardinal of the Filipino Catholic Church asked citizens to protect the military leaders who defected from the regime, millions of Filipinos formed a human barricade between Marcos's troops and the officers, which led to further defections of military officers to the opposition movement (Zunes, 1999). Marcos was forced to go into exile, which ended his twenty-one-year kleptocratic rule (Hutchcroft, 1991; Morgenbesser & Pepinsky, 2019).

2.3.5 Failed Revolutions in Azerbaijan and Belarus

Under President Heydar Aliyev's rule, Azerbaijan was a repressive regime effective in dividing the opposition and demobilizing the population through violence. Azerbaijan is a resource-rich country that depends on oil and gas for the bulk of its export earnings. Government positions were filled through cronyistic ties and bribery, and the high proportion of state-related employment allowed the regime to control society (Bunce & Wolchik, 2011, pp. 178–180). After the rigged election of 2003, a peaceful march organized by the opposition party leaders led to violent clashes with the police. The regime cited protestor violence to justify a massive crackdown on the opposition, resulting in hundreds of arrests. No single opposition leader could unite the opposition forces, which allowed the regime to continue its crackdown following the 2005 election (Bunce & Wolchik, 2011, p. 183). In addition, Russia had a strong interest in sustaining Aliyev's regime to balance against Western influence in the region. Meanwhile, the US was not interested in pursuing regime change in Azerbaijan due to strategic considerations of energy supply (Bunce & Wolchik, 2011, pp. 186–187).

Like Azerbaijan, Belarus gained independence after the dissolution of the Soviet Union in 1991. President Alexander Lukashenko's regime did not hesitate to use violence and coercion against dissent, resulting in the disappearance of opposition leaders (Bunce & Wolchik, 2011, p. 199). After the successful revolutions in neighboring Georgia and Ukraine, Lukashenko took steps to prevent a revolution by consolidating his power, demobilizing the political opposition, and constraining civil society. Unlike Georgia and Ukraine, Belarus was an electoral autocracy rather than a competitive authoritarian regime. Between 2001 and 2006, the government shut down more than 100 civil society organizations (Bunce & Wolchik, 2011, p. 203). Lukashenko also used the government-controlled media to discredit the opposition and to portray the revolutions as foreign-instigated social chaos (Bunce & Wolchik, 2011, p. 201; Marples, 2006; Silitski, 2006).

Unlike in Azerbaijan, the US and EU actively supported regime change in Belarus in the lead up the presidential election in 2006. However, Western governments had little leverage over the regime incumbent. Despite the growth of trade with the EU, Belarus's economy was still largely reliant on Russia for subsidies and cheap energy supplies, which strengthened the Kremlin's influence over Belarusian politics (Bunce & Wolchik, 2011, p. 203). Leverage aside, these failed cases had fewer linkages with Western governments and actors compared to the successful "Color Revolutions" countries, thus reducing the chances of toppling autocratic governments (Levitsky & Way, 2006).

2.4 Conclusion

In these stolen election-mass mobilization interactions, fraudulent elections provided the political opportunity and moral outrage to rally society to take part in large-scale collective actions. However, fraudulent elections did not cause revolutionary changes per se; it is mass mobilization that garnered widespread support that eventually toppled the authoritarian regimes. However, some mass uprisings led to revolutionary changes, while others did not. This section has provided case-study evidence to illustrate the greater likelihood of success of nonviolent resistance movements, since they lower the barrier to participation and unite the opposition. By shoring up the power of the people and the opposition, and making the autocratic governments look weak, mass demonstrations – once they reached a critical mass – often led to elite defection. Accordingly, disintegration of the ruling elites further precipitated regime downfall. For autocratic regimes that have strong non-Western foreign sponsors, such as Russia, their lack of linkages with the West, and/or absence of Western leverage over them, appear to be key factors in their failure to topple the rulers.

3 Movement-rooted Regime Change: Broad-based Social Movements, Coalitional Politics, and Regime Change

In Section 2, I outlined how mass mobilization following stolen elections toppled authoritarian regimes in Eastern Europe and elsewhere. Rigged elections presented opportunities to mobilize people in mass uprisings that brought about revolutionary outcomes. In this section, I introduce another causal mechanism that explains how social movements can lead to the electoral defeat of the incumbent regime.[5]

This section makes three core arguments. First, a broad-based nonviolent movement has the functions of coalescing antiregime forces across elites and distinct population segments, mobilizing them into collective actions, and paving the way for formal coalition building. This type of social movement is necessary to effect regime change in pluralistic and divided societies, such as Malaysia, the empirical case under examination in this section.

Second, and more generally, the potential for an opposition coalition to defeat the incumbents can be traced back to the breadth and depth of the preceding social movement. Broad-based movements with strong roots extending into society, often forged in collaboration with civil society, are more likely to bring about opposition coalitions that are serious challengers to the incumbents.

Third, an opposition coalition requires leaders' credibility to win elections, and alliance cohesiveness, to not only score but also sustain an electoral victory. This is a high bar for pluralistic and divided societies where political parties tend to be organized by communal blocs. Under these circumstances, a political opportunity that raises antiregime sentiments and precipitates elite defection can be helpful in bringing about regime change.

The core arguments above apply to all competitive authoritarian regimes. Yet, pluralistic and divided societies often face stronger hurdles in cross-mobilizing divided segments of the population and elites, and in defeating the incumbents accordingly. I call them "high-bar countries." As well, a political opportunity favorable to the movement can be instrumental in increasing popular support for the opposition and elite defection from the incumbents to the opposition camp, which helps to bring about a regime change in the high-bar cases.

The scope condition for the theory of broad-based movements advanced here is these high-bar cases of pluralistic societies where political parties are organized by communal blocs. In these contexts, no single communal bloc or opposition party can amass sufficient votes to get elected on its own, particularly in plurality electoral systems. A broad-based social movement can, therefore, serve useful purposes in cross-mobilization and presenting a united front against the incumbents, significantly improving an opposition coalition's likelihood of electoral success. The scope condition suggests while this theory is

---

[5] This section builds on an earlier paper, "From Voice to Vote: Electoral Movement, Coalitional Politics, and Regime Change in Malaysia" (January 14, 2019). Abstract available here: https://papers.ssrn.com/sol3/papers.cfm?abstract_id=3868285

most relevant to the high-bar countries due to the very nature of contentious politics and the institutional arrangements necessary to defeat the incumbents, it can still apply to authoritarian regimes that fall outside the high-bar category and to cases with less stringent requirements on breadth or depth of social movements, effectiveness of opposition pacts, or advent of a political opportunity.

Using process tracing, I inductively build this theory using the case of Malaysia, which experienced an electoral change in 2018. The Bersih, or "Electoral Reform," movement allowed existing opposition elites to mobilize civil society, forge alliances with other antiregime forces, and take advantage of a major corruption scandal implicating the prime minister and his family. The broad-based social movement became a platform that united all those who were against the kleptocratic regime, and led to the formation of a credible and reasonably cohesive opposition alliance that defeated the incumbents. In addition, I illustrate that not all opposition alliances are capable or cohesive enough to engineer an electoral victory throughout a twenty-year period. It takes credibility for a coalition to convince the voters of its governing capacity, and cohesiveness to maintain the coalition pre- and postelection.

The outcome variable in Malaysia's case is electoral defeat of the ruling coalition by the opposition coalition. It is used interchangeably with electoral or regime change. It is a lower bar than democratization or liberalizing electoral outcome (Howard & Roessler, 2006), which requires an opposition coalition to sustain its power after electoral victory in order to carry out democratic consolidation.

3.1 From Movement to Opposition Alliance Formation and Regime Change

More often than not, elections help autocrats in hybrid or competitive authoritarian regimes stay in power. Elections in these regimes take place on an uneven playing field that favors the incumbents over opposition parties (Diamond, 2002; Levitsky & Way, 2002; Lust-Okar, 2006). With their control over state resources, autocrats can also manipulate rules that shape the media landscape, limit citizens' access to information, and increase the challenge of coordination between the opposition (Magaloni, 2006; Simpser, 2005). As Section 2 has illustrated, large-scale postelection antiregime protests help to overcome the coordination problem between opposition elites and civil society (Bunce & Wolchik, 2010; Howard & Roessler, 2006; Schedler, 2013). This section will illustrate that mobilizing the masses to stage antiregime protests in the preelection period can similarly overcome the coordination problem.

3.1.1 Theory-building Process Tracing

Here, I use process tracing to build a theory to explain how uncoordinated opposition elites and discontented masses can bring about regime change. Process tracing allows us to "identify the intervening causal process – the causal chain and causal mechanism – between an independent variable and the dependent variable" in a single case (Bratton & Van de Walle, 1997; George & Bennett, 2005). Theory-building process-tracing is an inductive method, which starts with empirical material, and uses the material to detect a causal mechanism whereby X is linked with Y (Beach & Pedersen, 2015, p. 16).[6] It seeks to build a theory to describe a causal mechanism generalizable outside of the specific case to a bounded context (Beach & Pedersen, 2015, p. 91).[7]

While the theory holds true for electoral authoritarian states in general, it is of particular relevance to countries with plurality electoral systems, where opposition parties cannot easily coordinate their votes to win a simple majority. Opposition parties in these contexts face the inherent challenge of mobilizing voters across disparate segments of society and becoming electorally competitive. As well, it is highly salient for pluralistic and divided societies where political parties – and by extension, voters – are organized into communal blocs, divided by ethnic, religious, or other social cleavages. The main contribution of this theory is the mechanism it proposes through which opposition elites and discontented masses can meet, forge informal partnerships, and build coalitions to credibly compete in elections when the opposition faces headwinds in defeating the incumbents.

3.1.2 Causal Mechanisms

Figure 3.1 presents the broad contour of the process that traces uncoordinated opposition elites to discontented masses (X) to regime change (Y), but there is a "black box" in between them. Figure 3.2 further presents a causal process by which a broad-based social movement (a) as the independent variable brings about a credible and cohesive opposition coalition (b), and regime change (d), as the first and second outcome variables, respectively. The mechanism from (a) to (b) illustrates how the informal politics of protests contributes to formal institutional building, while that from (b) to (d) informs on the nature of an opposition coalition necessary to effectuate regime change.

The mechanisms are as follows:

---

[6] However, theory-building often has a deductive dimension where researchers draw lessons from existing theoretical literature.

[7] Middle-range theory is in between grand, parsimonious theories and complex, descriptive narratives. See also George & Bennett (2005).

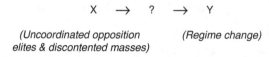

Figure 3.1 The "black box" in between "uncoordinated opposition elites & discontented masses" and regime change.

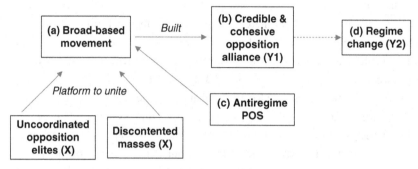

Figure 3.2 Regime-changing election through movement.
Source: Author's illustration.

(a) A broad-based social movement acts as a platform to coalesce opposition elites and discontented masses (X), and a mobilizing structure for collective actions against the regime;

(b) Movement rallies forge *informal* partnerships among opposition elites, civil society leaders, and would-be ruling party defectors, which serves as a stepping stone for *formal* coalition building (Y1);

(c) A broad-based social movement can aid in taking advantage of a political opportunity structure (POS) by uniting all antiregime elements into its fold. Despite not being a necessary condition, this can provide the impetus for an opposition victory when the bar of defeating the incumbents is extraordinarily high;

(d) The likelihood of bringing about a regime change (Y2) depends on the *credibility* and *cohesiveness* of the opposition coalition, facilitated by the broad-based social movement.

3.1.3 Theoretical Framework

Autocratic governments have the incentives and wherewithal to divide their opposition. The movement–election literature in authoritarian contexts has largely focused on how mass mobilization inspired by stolen elections has brought about revolutionary change (Beissinger, 2007; Bunce & Wolchik, 2012; Kuran, 1991; Tucker, 2007). This section offers a fresh perspective by underlining the functions of broad-based social movements that precede electoral competition. In other words, a movement per se does not lead to revolutionary change; it helps to forge unity among antiregime forces and build an opposition coalition strong enough to bring down the regime.

What are the utilities of a broad-based movement in removing autocrats from power? Such a movement can resolve disunity by coalescing all antiregime forces, inside and outside of institutional politics. In resource mobilization theory, mobilizing structures are a form of "collective vehicles, informal as well as formal, through which people mobilize and engage in collective action" (McAdam *et al.*, 1996, p. 3). Typical mobilizing structures, such as NGOs, clubs, churches, unions, professional associations, and informal networks, help movement entrepreneurs mobilize activists into collective actions. However, when movements become a means rather than an end, this study illustrates that a movement can in itself function as a mobilizing structure that unifies discontented masses and otherwise uncoordinated opposition elites, and mobilizes them into collective actions. In addition, large-scale cross-societal demonstrations help to signal the opposition movement's strength, or the incumbents' weakness. The palpable electoral defeat of the incumbent in turn mobilizes turnout of agnostic voters.

What qualifies as a broad-based movement? It is one that advocates for a cause shared across large swaths of society and identified by elites and nonelites alike. Such movement rallies are capable of mobilizing society beyond what NGOs and other typical mobilizing structures are able to do. Movements caused by stolen elections in the "Color Revolutions" are examples of broad-based social movements. Contemporary movements, such as Black Lives Matter, the Women's March, or the Occupy Movement, despite garnering supporters measured in the hundreds of thousands, still leave out sizeable out-groups. The Tea Party, Trump movement, and Alt-right movement are vocal movements that are far from being broad-based.

Further, movement rallies provide opportunities for opposition elites, movement entrepreneurs, and activists to regularly meet, and build rapport and informal networks. Rally participation can become a highly charged emotional experience that fosters a sense of camaraderie among protesters. The nature of social movements – as conflictual processes usually in confrontation with those in high political office – promote interpersonal bonds and coalitional networks (Diani & Bison, 2004).

Movements with a broad-based grievances also serve to coalesce potential regime defectors. The likelihood of toppling autocratic governments is higher with elite defection, such as those in the military, secret service, or coercive apparatus who are in the leader's inner circle (Bunce & Wolchik, 2011; Goldstone, 2001; Nepstad, 2011). Hence, a broad-based movement enhances the likelihood of a preelection regime split, thereby raising the likelihood of its downfall.

This study underscores the salience of brokers not only in social contention as McAdam, Tarrow, and Tilly (2001) have argued, but also in transforming contention into political institutions, namely, electoral opposition coalitions. Opposition elites who broker between political parties and a social movement can recruit disenchanted masses from across society, civil society organizations, and opposition groups to participate in the movement. Together, these movement participants make up a grand coalition of antiregime actors. As this section will demonstrate, brokers play a pertinent role in the inception of a broad-based movement, which is established with the aim of changing the rules of the (institutional) game.

This study also speaks to the literature on the importance of opposition coalitions for regime change (Bunce & Wolchik, 2012; Donno, 2013; Howard & Roessler, 2006; Ziegfeld & Tudor, 2017). The conditions for coalition formation matter – preelectoral coalitions are more likely to be formed among ideologically compatible parties and in disproportional electoral systems (Golder, 2005; Golder, 2006), but can be weakened by electoral repression and policy incongruency (Gandhi & Reuter, 2013; Gandhi & Ong, 2019).

Two characteristics of an opposition coalition – credibility of leaders and cohesiveness of the alliance – are particularly important in defeating the incumbents. A cohesive coalition *unites* opposition parties to compete under the same banner, instead of against each other, and *sustains* the alliance after it has won power. Preelection unity does not necessarily entail postelection sustainability. Instances abound of opposition coalitions falling apart after their hard-won victories. Leaders' credibility is pertinent for opposition elites to convince voters of their competence to govern once elected. This could be challenging in some authoritarian contexts where a long-ruling regime denies the opposition of any in-office experience. In these cases, the defection of ruling elites is necessary in lending credibility to the opposition's capacity to govern.

In countries where the opposition faces extraordinary challenges in defeating the incumbents, a political opportunity can provide the momentum needed to score a victory. As previously stated, political opportunities are exogenous factors that can manifest in the death of a revered political leader, succession crises that cause elite defection, shifts in international alliances, or corruption scandals shrouding and delegitimizing political leaders, which may lead to a sharp rise in antiregime sentiments (Meyer, 2004; Meyer & Staggenborg, 1996). A broad-based movement facilitates the rallying of antiregime forces arising from a political opportunity to attain the "threshold" for regime change.

Rising antiregime sentiments may also result in elite defection that helps to produce credible opposition leaders with in-office experience.

This study underscores the importance of the strategic choice of nonviolence in achieving successful outcomes by increasing the movement's mass appeal and sustainability (Chenoweth & Stephan, 2011; Sharp, 1973). In addition to reaffirming the existing literature that extols the merits of nonviolent resistance, this study extends the causal chain to explain its effects on changing electoral outcome.

This theory also speaks to the role of elite pacts in sustaining or destabilizing authoritarian regimes (Collins, 2002; O'Donnell *et al.*, 1986), and the importance of the social origins of institutional elite coalitions (Pepinsky, 2014). In *Ordering Power*, Slater (2010) traces the nature of contentious politics to the establishment of "protection pacts" among political elites, which determines the strength of authoritarian regimes. Violent insurgencies, he argues, pose threats for the elites and prompt them to set aside their differences to create strong ruling coalitions that in turn sustain authoritarian regimes. Examining cases from Southeast Asia, Slater argues that the violent conflicts in Malaysia in 1969 and in Indonesia in 1965 led to strong elite pacts that contributed to regime durability. This section argues contentious politics can *similarly* lead to elite coalitions – however, it is through a nonviolent movement that opposition elites forge informal partnerships, which cements an effective electoral coalition that effectuates a regime change. In other words, both studies similarly recognize the significance of the mechanisms of contentious politics and elite pacts in explaining the outcome variables of authoritarian regime change as well as durability. Incidentally, while Slater drew his theoretical insight from the 1969 racial riots in Malaysia, this section illustrates how nonviolent rallies led to opposition coalition building that eventually brought down the *same* regime more than sixty years later.

Further, a distinction should be made between electoral defeat of the incumbents and democratization or a liberalizing electoral outcome. While earlier studies have assumed formation of preelectoral coalitions to have liberalizing effects (Howard and Roessler, 2006; Bunce and Wolchik, 2011), recent works suggest defeats of the incumbent regimes may not necessarily result in democratization. Democratization is a long-term institution-building process, and the opposition's victory does not necessarily imply democracy has arrived (Wahman, 2013).

3.2 Malaysia's Political Landscape: Ethnic Politics, Multiparty Coalitions, and Mahathir's Rule

3.2.1 Data and Methodology

This study draws on primary interview data and secondary literature to conduct process tracing from the emergence of social movements, to the building of opposition coalitions, and to electoral change. Inductively, it constructs a theory about how social movements build alliances among opposition parties, which leads to the incumbents' defeat, from process tracing empirical evidence over a twenty-year period from 1998 to 2018. I conducted primary interviews with the present and past leaders of the Bersih movement, political elites, activists, and independent analysts in person and online in 2018–2019.

When conceptualizing the mechanisms, each component – social movement, political opportunity, opposition alliance – should be seen as an individually insufficient but necessary part of the whole. In other words, each component has no independent existence in relation to producing the outcome variable; they are all integral components of a "machine" that produces the outcome (Beach & Pedersen, 2015). I also draw upon publicly available electoral data to analyze electoral outcomes and show vote and seat swings at each election over the period of 1998–2018.

3.2.2 Multiparty Coalitions, Cronyism, and the New Economic Policy

Malaysia is a constitutional monarchy, and a multiethnic, multicultural, and religiously diverse society, consisting of the dominant Malays (69 percent of the population), ethnic Chinese (23 percent), and Indians (7 percent). It has a federal system that is made up of thirteen states, eleven of which are in Peninsular Malaysia, and two on Borneo Island in East Malaysia. The Malays are largely Muslim, whereas the Chinese and Indians belong to multiple faiths, including traditional Buddhism, Taoism, and Hinduism, as well as Christianity. Ethnic cleavages are also reflected in occupations, class divides, and geographical distribution. Traditionally, the Malays lived in rural communities, engaging in agriculture and fishing, the Chinese were mainly employed in the modern urban economy, such as mining, industry, and commerce, and the Indians were hired as plantation workers (Crouch, 1996, pp. 14–15). Economic development and urbanization since the 1990s have changed the demographics to some extent. Some younger Malays have moved into the cities to take up jobs in commerce and the government bureaucracy, whereas rural Malays continue to work in agriculture and abide by traditional Islamic teachings. By and large, the Malays still have lower social mobility than the Chinese and Indians.

Political parties in Malaysia are organized along ethnic cleavages. After gaining independence from Britain in 1957, Malaysia had been ruled by the multiparty Barisan Nasional (BN) or National Front coalition, led by the

Malay UMNO party, until 2018. The UMNO was established in 1946 to defend the Malays' indigenous rights (Crouch, 1996, p. 17).[8] While it was a multiparty coalition, the National Front was not an alliance of equals: the UMNO had always been at the center of the coalition, dominating its relationship with the other ethnic parties, such as the Malaysia Chinese Association (MCA) and the Malaysian Indian Congress (MIC) (Crouch, 1996, p. 34).

The racial riots in 1969 that occurred as a result of electoral gains by the Chinese opposition party gave rise to Malays' perceived threat to their dominant position. Consequently, the ruling coalition co-opted various regional political parties to strengthen the "protection pacts" against further riots (Brownlee, 2007; Crouch, 1996; Slater, 2012). In the wake of the riots, the UMNO abandoned gradualist policies in favor of the New Economic Policy (NEP), an affirmative action program, to grant special privileges to the *bumiputeras*, or Malays. The policy, which applied to areas such as higher education admissions, bureaucratic positions, and public companies' shareholding structures, has led to systematic discrimination against non-Malays. Ironically, it has also widened income gaps between the rich and well-connected Malays who benefit from the privileges, and the poor Malays who continue to make up the lower strata of society (Jomo, 2011).

"Money politics," or the use of patronage to buy votes, has been an inherent feature of Malaysian politics. The BN alliance consistently relied on cronyism and redistributive politics favoring certain ethnic groups to cultivate patronage networks (Gomez, 1991; Gomez & Jomo, 1997; Hicken, 2011; Searle, 1999).[9] Government projects were awarded to favored corporations in exchange for their political support. The close nexus between politics and cronyism had become a defining feature of Malaysia under Mahathir Mohammad, the strongman who led the country for twenty-two years from 1981 to 2003. Despite the economic boom under Mahathir's leadership, he was also known for despotism and coercion of rivals, and precluded them from forming a credible opposition. This had no doubt contributed to the durability of the UMNO regime, despite regular competitive elections (Pepinsky, 2007; Slater, 2003).

---

[8] Most of the first generation of UMNO leaders were part of the English-educated administrative elites that served the British colonial government.

[9] Accordingly, when the opposition successfully dissociated clientelism from political patronage, by capitalizing on voters' frustrations with government corruption, it was able to make substantial gains in the 2013 general election. See Weiss (2016).

3.2.3 The Asian Financial Crisis, Anwar's Dismissal, and the Reformasi Movement

Against the backdrop of the Asian Financial Crisis of 1997–1998, where political uprisings brought down the Suharto regime in neighboring Indonesia, politics in Malaysia entered a new era. Despite rapid economic growth, there was growing recognition of corruption, cronyism, and nepotism (KKN) in the government. Even though a middle class had emerged under Mahathir's rule, economic transformation had also eroded traditional Islamic values, increased income inequality, and enabled upward mobility of *only* a small segment of the well-connected population, while a sizeable proportion continued to be denied economic opportunities, especially in rural areas.

In September 1998, Mahathir sacked his deputy and heir-apparent, Anwar Ibrahim, on what were widely considered trumped-up charges of corruption, sodomy, and adultery, all of which were offenses punishable under Malaysian law. Anwar was believed to have fallen out of favor with the long-time autocrat.[10] A charismatic leader, and a former student activist with Islamic credentials, Anwar was popular among the younger Malay middle class.[11] Anwar started the Reformasi (reformation) movement, modeled after a similar grassroots political campaign demanding good governance and civil liberties in Indonesia in 1997–1998. After his detention, the Reformasi movement evolved into a "Justice for Anwar" (Keadilan) movement.

The movements brought together an array of organizations and individuals, including Islamic and secular NGOs, trade unions, student activists, the Islamic political party (PAS), the Chinese-dominated Democratic Action Party (DAP), and the newly set-up National Justice Party (Keadilan, or PKR) led by Anwar's wife (Weiss, 2006, pp. 15–16). The series of Reformasi rallies in 1998 typically attracted a few thousand participants, and up to 10,000 at their height (The Irish Times, 1998). Most of the supporters were Malays, with some limited involvement from the other ethnic groups. Yet, the Malay community remained divided over Reformasi – it had strong support from urban Malay youths and Muslim groups, but visible opposition in rural areas (Funston, 2000). Thus, despite being an unprecedented social movement at that point in time, the basis of support for Reformasi was rather narrow, as it drew support largely from urban Malays who were pro-Anwar and concerned with the human rights and

---

[10] There were policy differences between them. Anwar, who served as finance minister in Mahathir's cabinet, advocated IMF-style measures, going against Mahathir's preference for capital control during the financial crisis.

[11] To the younger Malay middle class, Anwar embodied a new generation of socially progressive Muslim leaders who embraced economic modernization, and yet was relatively uncorrupt. See Gomez & Jomo (1997).

governance issues of Mahathir's leadership. As the next section will illustrate, the nature of the Reformasi movement had a direct impact on the breadth and depth of the opposition alliance it forged, as well as its electoral outcome.

3.3 Interactive Dynamics Between Social Movements, Electoral Coalitions, and Outcomes Leading Up to the 2004 General Election

Given the communal orientation of political parties, coalition building has become a precondition for electoral contestation in Malaysia, since no single party can form a government on its own. The challenge of opposition coordination takes on even greater saliency in Malaysia, owing to its multiethnic makeup. The perennial challenge between the Chinese DAP and the Malay Islamic PAS has been to put aside their ideological differences for a united coalition to emerge. The authoritarian regime also presented a hurdle for either the opposition parties or civil society to effect any systemic political changes, as their individual uncoordinated actions were likely to be thwarted and impacts limited (Weiss, 2006, pp. 5–6; Giersdorf and Croissant, 2011, p. 9.). Table 1 details various movement rallies, opposition alliances, and corresponding electoral outcomes from 1998 to 2018.

The Reformasi movement in 1998 laid the foundation for a civil society–opposition party alliance (Weiss, 1999). After the movement, leaders from the DAP, PAS, and PKR formed the opposition coalition, Barisan Alternatif, which competed in the 1999 election.[12] The PKR is a majority Muslim party, but it is also multicultural in its composition. Its party elites were former NGO activists, former UMNO elites close to Anwar, and members of the Malaysian Islamic Youth Movement. Despite the multiethnic makeup of the Reformasi-facilitated alliance, the ties that held the various civil society groups and opposition parties together remained relatively tenuous. The priorities this coalition held in common were largely concerning Mahathir's treatment of Anwar, corruption, and Islam's emphasis on moral accountability (Jones, 2000).

The 1999 general election saw a drop in Malay support for the UMNO, causing the ruling coalition to lose a two-thirds majority of the popular vote for the first time. Nevertheless, the ruling National Front maintained power in part due to the success of the Chinese-MCA and regional parties in the state of Sarawak (Figure 3.3).[13] The results revealed some Malays' disapproval of Mahathir, particularly his treatment of Anwar, and with corruption associated with the

---

[12] The PAS's stronghold is in the northern states of Kelantan and Terengganu where it has maintained a network of Islamic schools and religious leaders, right down to the village level.

[13] Though it had managed to secure 76.7 percent of parliamentary seats in the first-past-the-post system, thanks to gerrymandering, its popular vote share fell to 56.5 percent (Chin & Wong, 2009).

Table 3.1 Movement rallies, opposition alliances, and electoral dynamics.

Movement Rallies	Opposition Alliance[1]	Elections
1998: Reformasi rallies with up to 10,000 participants.	Barisan Alternatif: DAP, PAS, & PKR.	1999: BN lost two-thirds of the popular vote for the first time.
2007: Bersih 1.0 rally with 40,000 participants.	Barisan Alternatif: DAP, PAS, & PKR. Pakatan Rakyat: PKR, DAP, & PAS.	2004: Landslide victory for BN. 2008: BN lost two-thirds majority of parliamentary seats. Beginning of the decline of MCA, Gerakan, & MIC.
2011: Bersih 2.0 rally with 50,000 participants. Global Bersih rallies in thirty-two cities worldwide.		
2012: Bersih 3.0 rally with 300,000 participants. Protests also held in ten other Malaysian cities and across thirty-four countries.	Pakatan Rakyat: PKR, DAP, & PAS.	2013: BN lost popular votes for the first time. Opposition alliance gained control of Selangor, Penang, & Kelantan. Record high voter turnout at 85%.
Aug 2015: Bersih 4.0 rally with 500,000 participants, riding on anger against 1MDB scandal that broke out in July 2015. Mahathir made first appearance at rally.		

November 2016: Bersih 5.0 rally held. Mahathir appeared at rally wearing yellow Bersih T-shirt.

Pakatan Harapan: PKR, DAP, Bersatu, Amanah. Mahathir and other senior Malay leaders defected from UMNO.

May, 2018: BN lost; PH won majority seats and formed government. Voter turnout at 83%.

1. Does not include small regional parties.

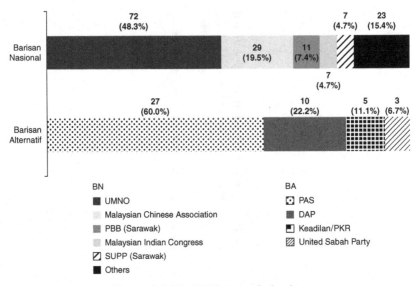

Figure 3.3 The 1999 general election.
(Number of seats; % within coalition, in parentheses.)
Popular vote: BN 56.5%; BA 40.2%.
Source: Election Commission of Malaysia.

UMNO. However, the bulk of the anti-UMNO Malay vote was redistributed to the PAS, rather than the Anwar-inspired party, PKR. The nascent party, PKR, had the smallest share among the opposition parties, trailing behind the PAS and DAP (Figure 3.3).[14] The PKR's lackluster electoral performance could be traced back to the relatively narrow support base of the Reformasi movement, which was heavily centered on young, middle-class Malay men, and lacked resonance with rural Malays and non-Malays (Noor, 1999; Weiss, 2006, pp. 133–134). It became evident that none of the Reformasi-championed causes or the Asian Financial Crisis was sufficient to vote the ruling coalition out of office.

In 2002, the DAP had a falling out with the PAS when the latter introduced *hudud* laws, an Islamic criminal justice system, in the states of Kelantan and Terengganu, where it governed.[15] This caused the opposition coalition to fall apart. Even though the two parties patched up their differences sufficiently to compete under the same banner in subsequent elections, significant divergence between them persisted (Interview with Steven Gan, editor-in-chief, *Malaysiakini*,

---

[14] The opposition alliance was rather unbalanced in weight: the PAS won twenty-seven seats (an increase of seven seats), while the DAP won ten seats (an increase of only one seat) (Chin & Wong, 2009).

[15] Such laws that impose restrictions on civil liberties based on religious piety would apply to all Muslims, but not to non-Muslims. The DAP opposed passing of the laws in principle. See Liow (2009); Noor (2014).

personal communication, July 2018). Although the coalition was unsuccessful, the dynamics between the 1998 Reformasi movement and the 1999 general election became the *first* of what McAdam and Tarrow (2011) term "cycles of electoral contention" in Malaysia. The recurring movement–election links became increasingly visible in rallies held in the second half of the 2000s and into the 2010s.

When Mahathir retired from politics in 2003, his successor, Abdullah Badawi, presided over an anticorruption campaign and delivered a landslide victory for the ruling coalition the following year.[16] BN's popular vote total rose to 64 percent from 56 percent previously, with better performance registered by almost all parties in the ruling coalition (Figure 3.4). Conversely, the opposition alliance's popular vote share almost halved from 40 percent to 24 percent.[17]

3.4 The Bersih Movement and Regime Change in Malaysia

3.4.1 The Bersih Movement

The 2004 election became an *inflection point* in the opposition coalition's struggle to engineer regime change. The National Front's outstanding gains underscored the *low* likelihood of a victory without electoral reform (Khoo, 2014b, p. 113; C. H. Wong, personal communication, July 2018). District boundary manipulation by the BN-controlled Electoral Commission had consistently disadvantaged the opposition parties. BN's strongholds were largely rural seats with low population density, while those of the opposition were typically urban districts with higher population concentration (Ostwald, 2013). District boundary delineation had an ethnic dimension – while poorer Malays are concentrated in rural villages, middle-class Chinese populate the metropolitan cities with lesser representation.

Elite-initiated Movement

Working together with twenty-five civil society organizations, opposition elites from the DAP, PAS, and PKR launched the Bersih movement, which stands for the "Coalition for Clean and Fair Elections," in 2006.[18] Bersih was preceded by the Joint Action Committee for Electoral Reform (JACER), launched in July 2005, which represented the opposition parties' first attempt in advocating for electoral reforms (Ooi, 2012). However, the JACER did not gain much

---

[16] In its best electoral performance since 1978, the ruling alliance won 64 percent of the popular vote and 90 percent of the parliamentary seats, and regained control of Terengganu state. See Liow (2004).

[17] The number of PAS seats dropped from twenty-seven to twelve and PKR's fell from five to one, which left the DAP as the largest party within the coalition.

[18] Its elite-initiated nature is not a necessary condition for developing a broad-based movement.

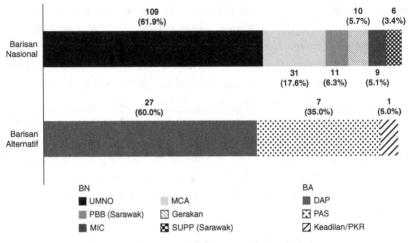

Figure 3.4 The 2004 general election.
(Number of seats; % within coalition, in parentheses.)
Popular vote: BN 63.9%; BA 24.0%.
Source: Election Commission of Malaysia.

traction, and opposition elites soon decided to pursue the agenda of electoral reform by forming a coalition with NGOs – which was the genesis of the idea for Bersih.[19] At the time of conception, the Bersih secretariat was driven by Research for Social Advancement, a pro-DAP organization directed by the DAP politician Liew Chin Tong, who was the party's key political strategist. This implied that Bersih was a social movement initiated and driven by the elites in the inception phase. The group of opposition elites involved in Bersih's founding included Liew Chin Tong and Teresa Kok (of the DAP), Sivarasa Rasiah and Tian Chua (of the PKR), and Mohammad Sabu and Dr. Dzukifly (of the PAS).[20] Among the NGO leaders, the key members were Maria Chin-Abdullah and Wong Chin Huat. Later, the Bersih founders reached out to the former president of the Malaysian Bar Council, Ambiga Sreenevasan, to lead Bersih 2.0 in 2011. By stepping down from the movement's leadership, the opposition elites faded behind the scenes in the NGO-led Bersih 2.0 and subsequent rallies.

These efforts amounted to attempts by the opposition elites, as institutional actors, to engineer an *extra-institutional* social movement, in collaboration

---

[19] The first NGO activists who worked with the opposition elites were Maria Chin-Abdullah of the Women's Development Collective, Yap Swee Seng of Suaram, Sonia Randawa of the Center for Independent Journalism, and Wong Chin Huat of the Writer Alliance for Media Independence. Source: Written communication with Wong Chin Huat, September 23, 2018.

[20] My communication with other interlocutors suggests the group membership might have been larger than indicated, but this list contains the core opposition elites who were involved.

with NGOs, that pushed for *changing the rules of the game* to allow for fairer *institutional outcomes*. Liew and other political elites straddled between their respective political parties and the social movement they created. Following the lukewarm response to the elite-driven JACER, the creators of Bersih emphasized forging coalitions with grassroots NGOs to gain support for the electoral movement. After passing the baton onto NGOs to lead Bersih, these elites migrated back to institutional politics. Put simply, they were political entrepreneurs with one foot in the party system, the other foot in the movement space, and they moved seamlessly between the two. As such, they brokered between institutional and civil society domains, and rallied and recruited new political actors committed to effectuating social change, such as A. Sreenevasan, Chin-Abdullah, and Wong.[21] The brokerage concatenated various mechanisms illustrated in Figure 3.2 that involves the establishment of a broad-based movement to galvanize across-the-board support from discontented masses, civil society organizations, and elites, which subsequently helped build effective opposition coalitions capable of changing political outcomes.

The Universality of Electoral Reform

Besides being germane to the rules of the voting game, electoral reform also serves a *tactical* purpose for the movement. To rally people behind an effective united front, the movement needs to advocate a grievance with which the people can identify and empathize. Identifying such a broadly shared grievance is no easy feat in a pluralistic society. With the post-Reformasi BA alliance falling apart not long after its formation,[22] people often wondered what it would take to cement the Bersih movement: "Can a predominantly non-Malay and secular DAP, a multiethnic PKR with a majority-Malay/Muslim leadership, and an ulama-led Malay/Muslim PAS form a coalition that would not be torn apart by ideological differences?" (Khoo, 2018, p. 478). As well, Bersih needed to reach into civil society and the populace, beyond the political elites. In the wake of the National Front's landslide victory in 2004, electoral reform was seen as a universally shared goal among the elites and masses (Liew, 2013).

Consequently, Bersih became a product of elite mobilization of civil society, and by extension, the masses, to pursue the opposition's political goals (Khoo, 2014a). To both the opposition and civil society, Bersih provided a common platform to bring together various groups – *inside* and *outside* of formal political

---

[21] The term "brokered" here takes on the same meaning as in McAdam, Tarrow, and Tilly (2001), which describes brokerage as one of the mechanisms of social contention.

[22] The Barisan Alternatif (BA) fell apart because of rifts between the DAP and PAS when the latter attempted to establish an "Islamic state."

institutions – to rally behind the shared objectives of fair elections and improved integrity of public institutions.[23] In contrast to Reformasi, which revolved around the themes of Islam and "justice for Anwar" (and later evolved into a broader theme of good governance), Bersih was secular and not focused on a parochial issue. Its more inclusive agenda garnered greater support across ethnic groups, classes, and geographical boundaries.

Strategic Choice of Nonviolence

> Despite being a non-democracy, Malaysians do not live in an oppressed society. No one is poor or desperate enough to take up arms or sacrifice their lives to bring down the government.
>
> Maria Chin-Abdullah, the leader of Bersih 5.0 (personal communication, July 2018)

In no small part, Bersih's capacity to rally huge crowds and sustain its collective actions is attributable to the strategic choice of nonviolence (Chenoweth & Stephan, 2011). With the exception of responses to the police's use of detention, teargas, and water cannons to break up protests,[24] and the threat of violence issued by right-wing Malay groups in later rallies (The Star, 2015), Bersih demonstrators had by-and-large adopted a nonviolent approach. With a per capita GDP of US$9,945, Malaysia is a middle-income country.[25] Tellingly, the earlier quote provided by Maria Chin-Abdullah revealed why middle-income Malaysians were not interested in a violent approach. She further elaborated, "after the rallies, people headed to their favorite *mamak* stalls, *kopitiam* or Coffee Beans."[26] This speaks not only to the multiethnic nature of the participation, but also the attitude of treating nonviolent protest as a social event, particularly for earlier rallies.

Bersih did not espouse a radical strategy to achieve its movement goal of free and fair elections, but advocated for change through universally respected institutional channels of reforming the electoral commission. Regime change did not feature in Bersih's lexicon until the exposé of the prime minister-linked corruption scandal in 2016.

---

[23] In contrast, the previous Reformasi movement drew disparate groups from the NGOs and opposition parties to pursue the agenda of seeking justice or *keadilan*, a process which Weiss describes as "coalitional capital bridged collectivities." See Weiss (2006, p. 6).

[24] Teargas and water cannons had been deployed against demonstrators since Bersih 2.0. See Alibeyoglu (2012).

[25] Data refer mostly to the year 2017 (The World Bank, 2017).

[26] *Mamak* stalls are local economical Indian eateries, *kopitiam* are local traditional coffee shops, whereas Coffee Beans is a more upscale Western-style coffee chain.

3.4.2 Causal Mechanisms

I employ process tracing to track the causal mechanisms between each set of Bersih rally–election interactions from 2007 to 2018. The 2018 electoral change was not brought about by any opposition coalition. The interactions between rally and opposition coalition first appeared in 1998–1999, but it did not defeat the ruling coalition. To effectuate regime change, the opposition coalition must possess two attributes: credibility and cohesiveness. Falling short of one or both of these qualities, the opposition coalition is not able to defeat the incumbents; and if it wins power, it will be an electoral turnover short of full regime change.

Credibility is operationalized by the credentials of opposition leaders, such as their social standing and previous government leadership experience, which serve as indicators for their governing competence. Cohesiveness is operationalized by common values or policy principles that hold the coalition together, which indicate whether the parties come together merely for the purpose of defeating the incumbents or to pursue a unified agenda once elected.

Bersih 1.0 and the 2008 Election

Process tracing arrives at two central arguments about electoral changes in Malaysia. First, as a broad-based movement, Bersih coalesced a wide range of civil society organizations and uncoordinated opposition elites. It was a social movement that advocated for electoral reforms, or simply "clean elections," a cause with which most Malaysians identify and sympathize. Unlike the Reformasi movement that revolved around Islam and "Justice for Anwar," Bersih was able to draw support from a relatively *broader* spectrum of society – beyond the Malay community and across different regions. Movement rallies facilitated interactions among political leaders from the DAP, PAS, and PKR, who shared few similar values but were united by the common objective of bringing the ruling coalition to an end. Informal cooperation during movement rallies helped to build formal opposition coalitions.

Second, collaborative efforts among opposition parties paid off in terms of their advancement against the ruling coalition at each electoral competition since Bersih's inception in 2007. The pertinent role of a broad-based movement in building opposition alliances should not be underestimated. Deeply divided along religious, ideological, and ethnic cleavages, the disagreements between the PAS and DAP are stark and irreparable in many respects. Yet, they came together in the social movement. Among the Bersih 1.0 elite leaders were the DAP's Liew Chin Tong and Lim Guan Eng, the PAS's Mohammad Sabu and Wan Azizah, and the PKR's Tian Chua. After the Bersih 1.0 rally, the three major opposition parties decided to reconcile their differences, and formed the

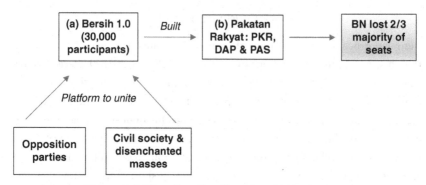

Figure 3.5 From Bersih rally 1.0 to 2008 election.

opposition alliance, Pakatan Rakyat, to compete in the upcoming election. The PKR in turn acted as a moderator between the Chinese DAP and Islamic PAS.

> Conservative leaders at PAS have been a strong advocate for an Islamic state, while DAP has always maintained the principles of multi-racialism and social democracy. Bersih provided an opportunity for the moderates and younger leaders from PAS and DAP to convince the conservative elements from their respective camps that it is acceptable to work together, in that they need not compromise their values.
>
> A key opposition leader of Bersih 1.0 stated (Personal communication,
> July 2018)

The first Bersih rally in November 2007 attracted 40,000 marchers to the National Palace in Kuala Lumpur, who conveyed to the king the imperative of electoral reform (Lee, 2007; Wong, 2005).[27] Smaller demonstrations organized in conjunction with Bersih 1.0 showed the widespread support from civil society, including a Bar Council-organized march against political appointments of Supreme Court judges (Chin & Wong, 2009, p. 78), and a Hindu Rights Action Force (HINDRAF)-organized assembly advocating for rights protections for ethnic Indians (Lee, 2007) .

The participants of Bersih 1.0 were mostly ethnic Malays and Indians; the ethnic Chinese were traditionally averse toward street politics due to the memory of the 1969 race riots (Interview with an opposition leader who led Bersih 1.0, personal communication, July 2018). As a barometer for Malays' support for the opposition movement, readership for the Malay edition of *MalaysiaKini*, the country's first independent news outlet, increased by three-fold leading up to the 2008 election (Interview with Steven Gan, editor-in-chief

---

[27] The Bersih 1.0 coalition of the opposition parties and civil society petitioned the king for reforms to the electoral system, which unfairly disadvantaged the opposition.

of *MalaysiaKini*, personal communication, July 2018). The racial dynamics, however, changed in the subsequent rallies.

Despite the lack of success for the opposition alliance in the 2008 election, the ruling coalition lost its two-thirds majority of parliamentary seats, which was an unprecedented outcome. The ruling coalition's share of the popular vote declined from 63.9 to 51.4 percent, and its share of parliamentary seats from 90 to 63 percent (Figure 3.6). The decline in support for the ethnic Chinese and Indian parties within the ruling coalition, the MCA and MIC, respectively, was particularly striking. While the UMNO's seats declined by 30 percent, the MCA and MIC saw their parliamentary seats more than halved. The National Front's win relied, more than ever before, on the gerrymandered rural districts of the regional parties in Sarawak, which contributed about 20 percent of total seats.

The opposition alliance, Pakatan Rakyat, won an unprecedented level of the popular vote at 47.4 percent, as well as eighty-two parliamentary seats, taking the majority in five out of thirteen states (Figure 3.6).[28] The PKR won the most seats within the coalition, followed by the DAP and PAS. Overall, the election held after the first Bersih rally shifted sizeable votes and seats away from the ruling coalition.

This quote from a prominent grassroots activist, Hishamuddin Rais, aptly captures the spirit of Bersih for civic solidarity (Khoo, 2014b, pp. 116–117).

> The strength of the Bersih movement is that people understood that they were cheated. Since the 1960s' elections, people have known that they were cheated. Suddenly, an organization comes out and tells them, it's okay for us to come together and show solidarity. So that is why Bersih was popular.

This interview quote from a key opposition leader of Bersih 1.0 speaks to Bersih's capacity to unite the elites and the masses.

> Bersih allowed the opposition elites to bring the civil society into its fold, so that it was no longer an elite-centered action, but one of a mass movement. And, we all rallied behind the shared goal of an electoral reform.

The 2008 election marked the beginning of the demise of the non-Malay parties in the ruling coalition – the MCA, Gerakan, and the MIC – and their once-formidable stronghold in electoral politics.[29] The UMNO-dominated ruling coalition had consistently marginalized the other coalition partners,

---

[28] They were the states of Penang, Kedah, Kelantan, Selangor, and Perak.

[29] The ethnic Chinese and Indian minorities have long harbored race-based grievances since the introduction of the affirmative-action program NEP in 1971. The NEP was succeeded by the New Development Policy in 1991, but the thrust of the policy remained largely the same.

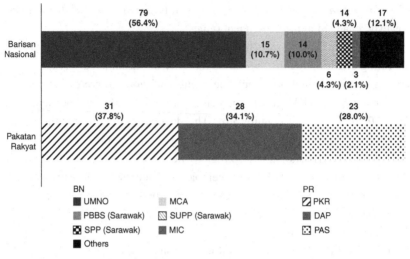

Figure 3.6 The 2008 general election.
(Number of seats; % within coalition, in parentheses.)
Popular vote: BN 51.4%; PR 47.4%.
Source: Election Commission of Malaysia.

leading to inadequate representation of the interests of ethnic minorities, namely the Chinese and Indians (Chin, 2001).[30] The non-Malays felt further marginalized after 9/11, when the issue of political Islam became more salient.

Yet, grievances did not automatically translate into votes. The opposition had to present itself as a strong enough alternative to the incumbents to persuade people to vote for them en masse. The large-scale alliance the opposition parties had forged with a wide array of civil society organizations – on display at the Bersih rally – signaled strength. All wearing bright yellow Bersih T-shirts, the 30,000-strong crowd that congregated at the Merdeka Square (Independence Square) symbolized the united strength of the antiregime forces, even though the movement was not explicitly framed against the regime.[31]

The opposition's strength may have been insufficient to defeat the incumbents in 2008, but it deprived the ruling coalition of its two-thirds majority of seats for the first time in history. This represented a significant improvement

---

[30] The Chinese's loss of the powerful finance minister portfolio after the NEP's introduction became a substantive and symbolic gesture of their diminished influence in politics.

[31] The rally also raised public awareness of unfair electoral procedures. Mobilization for the rally was conducted largely through social media, such as Facebook and WhatsApp. Combined with the rise of independent online media outlets, such as *MalaysiaKini*, new media channels began to end the government's monopoly on information dissemination, particularly among younger and better educated citizens in urban centers. See Pepinsky (2013) and Weiss (2013).

from the Reformasi movement in the 1999 election, when the incumbents won less than two-thirds of the popular vote for the first time. The distinction between the two electoral outcomes stemmed from the wider cross-sectional support Bersih had rallied compared to the Reformasi. This gave rise to a more cohesive opposition coalition in 2008, in terms of consolidated grassroots support across ethnic blocs and geographical regions, which translated directly into better electoral performance than a decade earlier. The only saving grace for the National Front was – thanks to gerrymandering – the strong win in the states of Sabah and Sarawak in East Malaysia, which effectively reduced it from a national coalition to an alliance between UMNO and East Malaysia's regional parties (Chin & Wong, 2009, p. 80).

Bersih 2.0

While the Bersih 1.0 movement was led by the elites, by 2011 the movement had become a civil society organization allied with the opposition. Bersih 1.0 was subject to criticism from government supporters for being too closely associated with the opposition parties (Interview with Maria Chin-Abdullah, a former leader of Bersih 5.0, personal communication, July 2018). In response, opposition leaders stepped down from Bersih's leadership positions in 2011, and were replaced by Ambiga Sreenevasan, a prominent human rights lawyer, as the leader of Bersih 2.0. The Bersih 2.0 rally held in 2011 attracted 50,000 participants in Kuala Lumpur, about a quarter more than the first rally. By then, Bersih had also transformed into a transnational movement. Global Bersih organized peaceful assemblies in over thirty countries in solidarity with the demonstrators at home (Lee, 2014), giving rise to a global "imagined community" of people in yellow T-shirts advocating for free and fair elections in Malaysia.[32] The large Malaysian diaspora community, estimated at 1.4 million and mostly composed of ethnic Chinese (The World Bank, 2011), hold sway in important swing constituencies (Gomez, 2013; Lee, 2014, p. 905).[33] The Global Bersih movement was successful in raising political awareness among Malaysians at home and abroad about their voting rights and the government's manipulation of electoral rules to its advantage (Khoo, 2016a; Lee, 2014).

---

[32] Bersih 2.0 put forward eight demands: (1) clean up the electoral roll; (2) reform postal ballot voting; (3) use indelible ink; (4) free and fair access to mass media for all parties; (5) minimum twenty-one days campaign period; (6) strengthen public institutions; (7) no corruption; (8) no dirty politics. Demands 1 to 4 had been formally advanced by Bersih 1.0.

[33] Among the host countries, about half a million work in neighboring Singapore, and about 150,000 Malaysians reside in Australia. About 750 people gathered at the 2011 Bersih rally in Melbourne, and the number of attendees increased to over a thousand in 2012.

Bersih 3.0 and the 2013 Election

Next, Bersih organizers held another rally, Bersih 3.0, in 2012 in anticipation of an election the following year. Corralling an even stronger coalition of eighty-four NGOs, including the national trade union, human rights organizations, the national bar council, environmental movements, and Islamic, Buddhist, Christian, Hindu, and Sikh NGOs, Bersih 3.0 attracted an estimated 300,000 participants in Kuala Lumpur, six times the size of Bersih 2.0.[34] Rallies were also held across the country, from Malacca, Ipoh, and Kuantan in Peninsular Malaysia, to Kuching, Miri, and Kota Kinabalu in East Malaysia.

The strong support for Bersih 3.0 had a manifold effect on the electoral outcome in 2013. The most palpable effect was voter mobilization: voter turnout rose from 73–75 percent in the 1999, 2004, and 2008 elections to a record high of 84.8 percent in 2013 (Figure 3.8). Various Bersih-related NGO campaigns that encouraged overseas Malaysians and those working in neighboring countries to return home or to cast ballots through postal voting delivered strong results (Khoo, 2016b). Consequently, the ruling coalition *lost the popular vote for the first time* in 2013 – yet another electoral advancement for the opposition. The significance of the Chinese MCA and Indian MIC parties in the ruling coalition continued to decline (Figure 3.9), but the National Front still managed to win 61 percent of seats. In no small part, this was attributable to the electoral win by the regional parties in Sabah and Sarawak, which contributed more than 20 percent of the coalition's total seats – and constituted yet another piece of evidence of the unfair advantage gerrymandering had delivered to the ruling coalition.

Despite gaining control of the states of Selangor, Penang, and Kelantan, it became exceedingly clear to the opposition that a multiethnic coalition, backed by strong civil society support, was still insufficient for defeating the incumbents (Lin, 2013; Lyn & Ding, 2013). None of the opposition elites – with the exception of Anwar – had any significant experience in government. Anwar returned to politics in 2008 as leader of the opposition, after an eight-year hiatus (1999–2007), including five years in jail. However, his political status remained precarious at that time, as he was handed another five-year jail sentence in 2014 for a sodomy charge, in what was widely believed to be Prime Minister Najib Razak's attempt to disqualify him from contesting the election (Subramaniam, 2014). The opposition lacked the credibility to convince the voters they could do a better job than the National Front, if elected. The opposition parties – the DAP, PAS, and

---

[34] Smaller rallies were held in ten other cities in Malaysia, and thirty-four countries across the world.

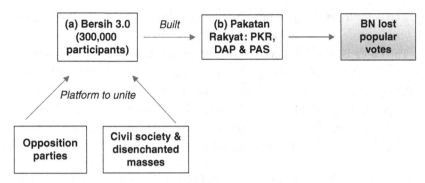

Figure 3.7 From Bersih rally 3.0 to 2013 election.

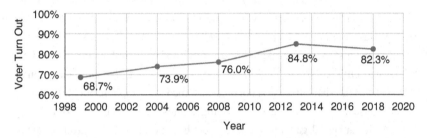

Figure 3.8 Voter turnout in Malaysia's general elections, 1999–2018.
Source: International Institute for Democracy and Electoral Assistance.

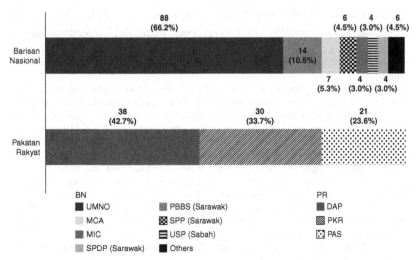

Figure 3.9 The 2013 general election.
(Number of seats; % within coalition, in parentheses.)
Popular vote: BN 47.4%; PR 50.9%.
Source: Election Commission of Malaysia.

PKR – came together again this time, on the platform of Pakatan Rakyat, but it was no more cohesive than it had been in the past.

The ruling coalition did not only benefit from the manipulation of electoral boundaries; there were also alleged problems of voter fraud associated with postal votes and indelible ink.[35] Further, popular programs introduced by Najib's government, such as 1Malaysia's discount grocery stores, 1Malaysia's medical clinics, and financial aid to the poor, had boosted the government's popularity among lower-income and rural households (Mahavera, 2015; Weiss, 2013).

Bersih 4.0

When the opposition appeared to have hit a brick wall, a massive corruption scandal surrounding the 1 Malaysia Development Berhad (1MDB), the country's sovereign wealth fund, broke out in May 2015.[36] This massive scandal involving US$3.5 billion in stolen funds, which the US Department of Justice (DoJ) has described as "the largest kleptocracy case" ever, put then-Prime Minister Najib Razak at center stage.[37] The tale of bribery interlaced with Hollywood stars and the "Malaysian Official No. 1"[38] infuriated the country at both the elite and popular levels. The Malaysian citizenry is not unaccustomed to corruption, but the scandal's gargantuan scale, Najib and his wife's profligate lifestyle,[39] and the lack of trickling down of the unlawful gains to the grassroots became the lightning rod of public wrath (Hope & Wright, 2018). In contrast to cronyism during Mahathir's high-growth era, embraced as part of the business and political culture, the 1MDB scandal enriched the most powerful family at the expense of the rest of the population, which faced slow economic growth and high inflation. The scandal moved Malaysia categorically closer to Ferdinand Marcos's kleptocratic regime in

---

[35] Anwar led a postelection movement of about 120,000 people wearing black to protest electoral fraud.

[36] The 1MDB, set up in 2009, was intended to promote economic development by seeking high investment returns. The scandal was known in financial circles for some years before journalists brought it to the world's attention. The UK investigative journalist, Clare Rewcastle Brown, who was born in Sarawak, maintains the website *Sarawak Report* – banned in Malaysia during Najib's rule – dedicated to exposing the political scandal. Two *Wall Street Journal* reporters, Tom Wright and Bradley Hope, further amplified it internationally. See Haynes (2018).

[37] The US DoJ has alleged that some 1MDB stolen funds had found their way to bank accounts associated with the former PM Najib Razak. The investment bank, Goldman Sachs, has also been implicated for its role in 1MDB's bond issuance. The scandal also involved Jho Low, a friend of Najib's stepson, and Riza Aziz, who produced the Hollywood blockbuster *The Wolf of Wall Street*, which starred Leonardo DiCaprio. For details of the corruption scandal and investigations, see Ramesh (2016).

[38] The US DoJ had referred to the corrupt mastermind as "Malaysian Official 1," without naming the former prime minister explicitly.

[39] It has been reported that Najib and his wife spent US$750,000 on flowers for the wedding of one of their children. After Najib's ouster, the police raided his residence and found his wife to be in possession of Birkin and other luxury handbags, jewellery, and cash worth US$273 million. See BBC News (2018).

the Philippines, and away from the newly industrializing country it had once been known as.[40]

> Malaysians are not unused to corruption. But, Najib had only shared a small fraction of the stolen funds with his supporters, about 10 percent of the US$680 million. This was what made the Malay community so angry; even his so-called "cronies" did not benefit from the stolen funds from state largesse. Interview with James Chin[41]

The exposé of the 1MDB scandal caused an eruption of pent-up resentment against the Najib government. It became a significant "political opportunity" – in social movement terms – for the Bersih movement. The Bersih 4.0 rally held in August 2015, three months after the scandal's exposé, attracted an estimated 500,000 participants – the largest gathering thus far.[42] It was supported by a wide range of civil society organizations, including the progressive Malay organizations IKRAM and ABIM, and the environmental organization Himpunan Hijau. The DAP and PKR also participated in the rally, though the PAS withdrew its support, accusing Bersih of being "anti-Malay" (Interview with Bersih Interim Executive Director, Shahrul Aman, personal communication, July 2018). Nevertheless, rally participants came from all racial backgrounds, including a 50:50 ratio between Malays and non-Malays.[43] The movement was still largely nonviolent, despite reported cases of police brutality and the government's more widespread use of tear gas and water cannons against protestors compared to the last rally (Ang, 2012). For the first time, the movement called for Prime Minister Najib's resignation (Malaysiakini, 2015).

Outraged by Najib's scandalous behavior, former Prime Minister Mahathir Mohammad, a long-time nemesis of the opposition and civil society, made an unexpected appearance at the rally – and was much cheered by the yellow-shirt demonstrators (SD Reporters, 2015). Thus, the Bersih 4.0 rally served as a platform to bring into its fold the political veteran and longest-serving prime minister, made possible by the 1MDB political opportunity. As a key political leader of Bersih 1.0 explained:

> Mahathir had indicated his intention of joining the opposition camp after the 1MDB scandal deepened over time. But, given his previous position (being a long-standing leader of the ruling coalition), you can imagine how his action

---

[40] During the 1980s and 1990s, Malaysia was held up as a second-tier Asian tiger, a coveted title given to the high-growth developing countries.

[41] A Malaysian political scientist based at the University of Tasmania, over Skype call, in November 2018.

[42] In addition, seventy Global Bersih rallies were also held around the world, showing solidarity for the demonstrators in Kuala Lumpur.

[43] This claim was made by the Malay newspaper, the *Malay Mail*. See Zahiid & Lin (2015).

might be perceived by the public if he were to cross over to the opposition right away. Bersih 4.0 provided a perfect entry point for him to legitimately join the rakyat (people) at the rally.

Bersih 5.0 and the 2018 Election

Political Opportunity: Corruption Scandal and Elite Defection

What was it about the movement–opposition coalition that brought about the electoral change in 2018? After all, there had been a number of rallies and opposition coalitions prior to that. The difference this time was the political opportunity of a massive corruption scandal that implicated the highest office-holder and his family, which fueled antiregime sentiments and spurred elite defection. This led to co-optation of former elites with significant in-office experience into Bersih, which paved the way for a credible opposition coalition. It should be underscored that elite defection, in itself, is insufficient to bring about the desirable outcome. In 1999, the defection of elites from the UMNO to PKR (coupled with the Reformasi movement) was incapable of bringing down the ruling coalition. A political opportunity was a necessary condition in Malaysia's case due to the significant hurdles of defeating the incumbents in a pluralistic society. The causal mechanisms from the movement, a credible opposition coalition, and electoral change are illustrated in Figure 3.12.

When news of the scandal broke, a group of UMNO veteran leaders either quit the party or were sacked by Najib for being too critical. Among them were Mahathir and then-Deputy Prime Minister Muhyiddin Yassin. This led to a widely held belief among the Malay elites that the UMNO – which once championed their interests – had lost its compass and legitimacy (Wan Jan, 2018). For the Malays, the unprecedented scale of 1MDB far exceeded the abhorrence of Mahathir's imprisonment of Anwar. For the first time since the Reformasi movement twenty years ago, a major political upheaval led to the Malay community's firm belief about the necessity for change. This conviction did not arise easily; after all, many Malays had been benefactors of the UMNO's pro-*Bumiputra* policy.[44]

After his exit from the UMNO, Mahathir led several other defected Malay elites to form Bersatu in September 2016, a new Malay-centric party that championed *Bumiputra's* privileges, a position the UMNO traditionally

---

[44] The Malay community is traditionally shaped by a deeply ingrained political culture that promotes respect for leaders, and disdain for those who "bite the hands that feed you." See Rahman (2018).

Figure 3.10 Bersih demonstration against the iconic Petronas Twin Towers.

occupied. To be sure, Bersatu was not the first UMNO splinter party. Yet, what differentiated it from the PKR in 1999 and Semangat 46 in 1987 was Mahathir's leadership. Having ruled the country for more than twenty years, and despite a slightly tainted record over the Anwar saga, Mahathir still enjoyed a mythical stature in the public sphere. He presided over a high-growth period that saw the expansion of the middle class, which juxtaposed starkly with the moribund economy and rampant corruption of Najib's tenure.

Mahathir Appearing at Bersih 5.0 Wearing a Yellow T-shirt

As the 1MDB scandal deepened, Bersih organizers put together Bersih 5.0 in November 2016. In what became the final mass rally before the historic election, the government's hardline repression of the movement increased. The police arrested scores of prominent activist leaders before and after the rally (Shahrul Aman, Bersih's interim leader, personal communication, July 2018).[45] A UMNO division chief organized a countermovement, the Red Shirts, consisting of hooligans trying to thwart the yellow-shirt Bersih supporters (Khoo, 2016a). A score of activists, including the Bersih leader Maria Chin-Abdullah and several DAP leaders, were arrested the day before the rally

---

[45] In addition, the government accused Bersih of taking money from the Jews, i.e. George Soros's Open Society Foundations, in a plot to topple the regime.

(FMT Reporters, 2016b; NST Online, 2016). Despite that, the planned Bersih 5.0 went ahead, but with a smaller crowd of 50,000 participants (Hew, 2016).

When Mahathir appeared at the rally once again – wearing the "official" yellow Bersih T-shirt and as Bersatu's leader this time around – the masses were exhilarated (FMT Reporters, 2016a). His presence signaled the veteran leader was now *officially* on the side of the opposition and civil society against the much detested kleptocratic government. Once again, the Bersih rally became the mobilizing structure that coalesced all anti-Najib forces, inside and outside institutionalized politics.

After the rally, Bersatu officially joined the opposition alliance, Pakatan Harapan (PH). Together with Amanah (a moderate splinter party from the PAS), Bersatu replaced the PAS to represent Malays' interests in the coalition to appeal to hardcore *Bumiputera* supporters. However, not all Bersatu party members agreed with its Malay nationalist agenda, particularly the young, who accounted for more than half of its membership.[46] Mahathir also worked out a deal with the PKR and DAP elites that he would lead the coalition into the election, but pass the baton to Anwar after a two-year transition period.

Bersih's Support Base

Even though Bersih built on the foundation of the civil society–opposition party partnership established by Reformasi two decades ago (Weiss, 2006), its support base surpassed the earlier movement by a wide margin. This made consequential differences on electoral outcomes. Bersih not only transcended ethnic groups, religions, and personalities, which defined Reformasi to a large extent, but it also had a wider geographical reach. By including the 1MDB scandal on its list of grievances, Bersih resonated with voters in the eastern states of Sabah and Sarawak, where Reformasi and the Anwar saga never had any real influence.

> No one was happy with the way the Najib government spent money, especially the luxurious lifestyle his and his family led. People here (in Sarawak) were angry enough to join Bersih rallies, a protest culture we have never really embraced. In contrast, the jailing of Anwar and the Reformasi movement had never affected us much. It was very much a Malay and Peninsular Malaysia issue.
>
> Interview with a Chinese newspaper editor in Sarawak (Kuching, Sarawak, personal communication, July 2018)

Granted, Bersih did not resonate in every corner of society. Its supporters were more urban than rural, more educated, and in the later rallies, more

---

[46] The Malay youths born in the 1980s, who came of age during Mahathir's high-growth era, have suffered an erosion in their standard of living due to Najib's mismanagement of the economy. See Wan Jan (2018, pp. 13–19).

Chinese than Malay. Yet, in a multiethnic and highly divided society, its support base was as broad as a movement could plausibly achieve.

Credibility and Cohesion of the Opposition Coalition

Credibility was an important consideration given the preelection economic context.[47] Rising inflation, stagnant growth, and the unpopular GST introduced by Najib's government gave rise to the urgency for a "clean government" that could create economic growth and generate employment.

Prior to 2018, the opposition coalitions were never cohesive in the first place. Often, political parties collaborated when they faced a common enemy. Other than the principle of electoral reform, they did not share similar values or policy principles. Bersatu was united with the DAP, PKR, and Amanah by their desire to purge the Najib kleptocratic government, above all else. This mirrored the long-standing mistrust between the PAS and DAP. As a Malay scholar writes, "A majority of Malays are always suspicious of Malay-dominated parties forming alliance with the DAP because of their fear of usurpation by the ethnic Chinese party" (Rahman, 2018).

With a high 82 percent voter turnout, the opposition coalition secured 55 percent of seats (48 percent of the popular vote), leaving the National Front with 36 percent of seats (34 percent of the popular vote), and the PAS, which competed independently, with 8 percent of seats. The PKR was the largest party in the coalition, followed by the DAP and Bersatu (Figure 3.13). The Chinese MCA and Indian MIC were nearly decimated in the election, continuing their decay since the launch of Bersih a decade earlier. Bearing the ultimate price of Najib's personal excesses, the UMNO suffered great losses, with its number of seats declining from eighty-eight to fifty-four. Tellingly, a slogan chanted in the Bersih 4.0 and 5.0 rallies was *Tangkap Najib, Hidup Rakyat!* (Capture Najib, Long Live the People!) With that, the Mahathir-led coalition won the election, ended the National Front's sixty-one-year rule, and brought an end to Najib's kleptocracy.

3.4.3 Post-2018 Political Changes

Two years after winning office and after a series of byelection losses, in March 2020, the PH government collapsed and placed in limbo the hope for political change that the historic 2018 election had ignited. Amidst high expectations following the election, economic growth remained slow and foreign investment only trickled in slowly. However, the most contentious issue was the power transition from the ninety-four-year-old Mahathir to his former

---

[47] On this point, this section takes the opposite position from Ufen (2020).

Figure 3.11 Mahathir Mohammed (in the middle) appeared in Bersih 5 rally clad in a bright yellow T-shirt.

Photo credit: Bersih.

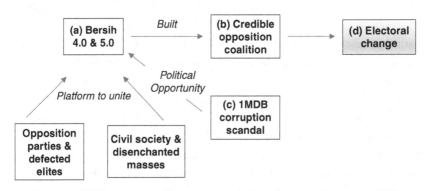

Figure 3.12 How the Bersih movement led to electoral change in 2018.

archrival, Anwar. In the two years after the election, Mahathir refused to confirm a date for the handover to Anwar, and instead groomed a leader from a rival faction of Anwar's PKR. Mahathir then suddenly tendered his resignation as prime minister to the monarch, to everyone's surprise, which led to the collapse of the coalition in office (Head, 2020). Though what went on behind the scenes at the so-called "Sheraton Hotel coup" is still far from clear (Roundup, 2020), it appears that Mahathir was outmaneuvered by his own deputy in Bersatu. Mahathir's deputy, along with Anwar's archrival, whom

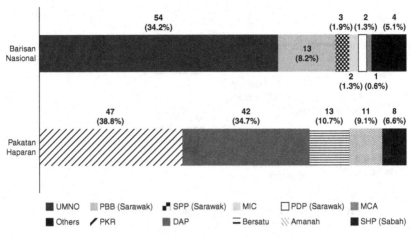

Figure 3.13 The 2018 general election.
(Number of seats; % within coalition, in parentheses.)
Popular vote: PR 48.0%; BN 33.8%.
Source: Election Commission of Malaysia.

Mahathir had been trying to groom, led their respective supporters to form another coalition. Together with the PAS, they constituted a new minority government without either Mahathir or Anwar – all without holding an election. The political drama happened while the country was under a COVID-19 lockdown that impeded efforts to organize any rallies (Paddock, 2020).

In light of these political developments, the 2018 election appears to be a case of electoral change without democratic consolidation (Diamond, 1999; Linz & Stepan, 1996; Schedler, 1998). It was not so much because of deficiencies in civil society, the rule of law, or factors that Linz and Stepan have argued are key for democratization (Linz & Stepan, 1996). Rather, it was due to a lack of elite consensus to choose democracy as a code of political conduct (Higley & Gunther, 1992), as some political elites chose to undermine democratic institutions through "backroom politics" in order to win power.

Democratic consolidation failed in this instance because the PH alliance, though credible, was not a cohesive coalition. The PKR, Bersatu, and the DAP shared few common political values or policy principles. Mahathir and Anwar decided to leave aside their long-term animosity momentarily because they faced the common, and worse, enemy of Najib's kleptocracy. Once Najib was ousted, acrimony and mistrust between them resurfaced, with the ultimate cost of power loss by the opposition alliance, despite their decades of struggle within and outside institutional politics to bring down the National Front regime. Yet, as noted earlier, Malaysia has never seen a truly cohesive opposition alliance, an

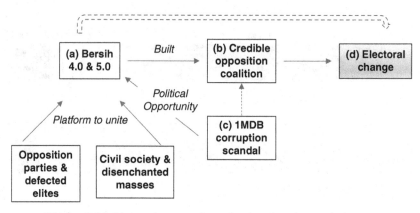

Figure 3.14 Alternative causal mechanisms to electoral change.

inherent product of the divided society and the long-ruling coalition's capacity to thwart dissent. Cohesiveness was necessary to win power, as well as to sustain power after electoral victory – which the opposition coalition could not accomplish.

3.4.4 Alternative Explanations

A central shortcoming of process tracing is its inability to mediate between alternative explanations. Here, I consider two alternative explanations that may account for the outcome, but I argue they are not as credible as the causal mechanism presented earlier.

First, could a political opportunity lead to electoral change directly without intermediating through a broad-based social movement? An oft-heard explanation of the 2018 election results was the 1MDB corruption scandal and the resultant "Mahathir factor" – that is, elite defection brought about by the scandal – which brought down the ruling coalition. This alternative mechanism is represented by the dotted arrow from (c) directly to (b), without going through (a), in Figure 3.14.

This explanation does not stand up to empirical scrutiny. The Bersih movement, in terms of its *capacity* to corral and unite all antiregime forces, its demonstration of the strength of antiregime sentiments, and its facilitation of the formation of an opposition coalition, was critical to Mahathir's formation of Bersatu and joining the PH alliance. After the scandal was widely reported by international press in July 2015 (Wright & Clark, 2015), Mahathir showed up at Bersih rally 4.0 in August in his personal capacity to join the people in calling for Najib's resignation (Kumar, 2015). In March of the following year, 2016, Mahathir quit UMNO, calling it "Najib's party" (Au, 2016). In August 2016,

together with the other former UMNO elites, Mahathir registered a new political party, Bersatu (FMT Reporters, 2016a). Again, Mahathir participated in
another rally, the Bersih rally 5.0 in November 2016 – this time in his official
capacity as the chief of the party, Bersatu (The Straits Times, 2016). At the rally,
he wore the bright yellow Bersih 5 T-shirt and called for people to "show
dissatisfaction with the government through (their) participation in the rally
by Bersih at Dataran Merdeka [Independence Square]" (The Straits Times,
2016). Mahathir was also seen wearing a "Free Anwar" badge, in support of
the leader of the PKR who was serving a jail sentence for what was believed to
be a politically motivated sodomy conviction (The Straits Times, 2016).
Subsequently, in December 2016, Bersatu officially entered into an electoral
pact with the PH coalition to compete against the National Front in the next
election (Harun, 2016).

In short, in the counterfactual scenario of the scandal leading directly to an
electoral pact between Mahathir's party and the PH coalition, Mahathir need not
have participated in two Bersih rallies – in joining the protestors to call for
Najib's resignation and appealing for greater participation in the mass movement. Hence, the role of the movement as a unifying platform for the antiregime
elites and masses, and as a stepping stone to formal coalition building, is *not*
inconsequential.

Second, could the corruption scandal have increased antiregime sentiments so
significantly that it led to mass votes against the ruling coalition, making the
formation of an opposition coalition inconsequential? If this alternative explanation
were true, it would be represented by the arrow from (c) to (a), and the dotted block
arrow from (a) to (d), bypassing formal opposition coalition (b), in Figure 3.14.

In this counterfactual scenario, let us take the rally size as an indicator of the
strength of antiregime sentiments. The Bersih 4.0 rally attracted approximately
500,000 participants – ten times larger than the estimated 50,000 in Bersih 5.0, the
rally immediately before the 2018 election. There was palpable "protest fatigue"
in the period between the two rallies: people in the streets were growing weary
and skeptical of whether their collective actions would ever bring about any
substantive change at the ballot box (Interview with Steven Gan, editor-in-chief,
MalaysiaKini, personal communication, July 2018). Granted, the turnout at the
Bersih 5.0 rally might have been negatively affected by the government's threat of
violence against demonstrators. However, it was still substantively smaller than
the 300,000-strong Bersih 3.0 rally that did not bring down the incumbents. Thus,
a broad-based movement per se, in the absence of a credible opposition coalition,
was an insufficient condition. The arrival of the political opportunity that resulted
in elite defection mediated through movement rallies, which led to the formation
of a credible opposition coalition, must be the consequential mechanisms in

effecting the 2018 electoral change. It was an outcome that neither social movement nor elite defection – on their own – could have achieved.

3.4.5 External Validity

To illustrate external validity, I draw on the cases of Kenya and Zimbabwe to apply the causal chain in Figure 3.1 that maps the mechanism from uncoordinated opposition elites and discontented masses to electoral change, with a "black box" in between. The "black box" consists of a broad-based movement capable of coalescing the elites and populace alike, signaling mass discontentment with the regime, and showing opposition strength. It also fosters informal partnerships among elites, and thus precedes the formation of an opposition coalition credible and cohesive enough to win power. On the one hand, Kenya demonstrates how the opposition coalition's lack of cohesiveness can be traced to the absence of a movement-origin and penetration into the grassroots, which is a reflection of its multiple-cleavage society. On the other hand, Zimbabwe elucidates an opposition alliance, strongly rooted in labor movements with deep linkages with the grassroots, capable of mobilizing support across society, even though its victory was beset by lack of governing experience.

Similar to Malaysia, Kenya is a pluralistic society with its politics ethnicized since the colonial era, where rulers relied on ethnic brokers and, later, ethnic associations to rule a divided society. This social structure rooted in colonial history created obstacles for cross-regional and cross-ethnic political mobilization (Anderson, 2005; Branch, 2006; Cheeseman, 2006; Orvis, 2006).

Despite prolonged fiscal crises since the late 1980s, President Daniel Moi in Kenya was adept at securing funding from international donors, while making little progress on economic or political reforms. Moi's KANU party centralized power, built party institutions in local communities, and expanded coercive controls throughout society. "Queue voting," introduced in 1986, undermined the secret ballot by requiring voters to line up behind their candidates of choice (Branch & Cheeseman, 2006). Protests driven largely by discontent with Moi's authoritarian government culminated in the formation of the opposition party, the Forum for Restoration of Democracy (FORD), when multiparty elections were allowed in 1992. However, since independence, the government had always co-opted or dismantled civil society organizations that might pose a threat to its rule. With a stifled civil society, the discontented masses and opposition elites lacked a mobilizing structure (LeBas, 2011, Chapter 6).

The FORD drew its support from urban-based movements, while the Catholic Church, though active in pushing for political reforms, had failed to connect with civil society at large. The fragmentation of society along ethnic lines, coupled with Moi's longstanding repression, had hindered broad-based or cross-societal mobilizing structures. Street protests, despite becoming increasingly frequent after 1990, turned into cycles of rioting and repression, rather than a sustained movement. The absence of networks to connect urban and rural constituencies, and across ethnic groups, not only resulted in uncoordinated protests, but also had a constraining effect on the strength of the opposition movement (LeBas, 2011, Chapter 6). Electoral violence that was ethnically driven further undermined cross-ethnic mobilization of support for the opposition parties (Mueller, 2008).

Within a month of the FORD's party registration, it split into two separate parties: FORD-Kenya, supported by the Luo tribe, and FORD-Asili, which drew on support from the Kikuyu and Luhya. Political elites had expended few resources to forge cross-ethnic linkages. Hence, ethnicity remained the key determinant of presidential vote choice despite the introduction of multiparty elections (Bratton & Van de Walle 1997). The Kenyan opposition parties were fragmented, and their candidates frequently defected and switched party labels, with little admonition from the electorates.

Despite that, opposition leaders were able to cobble together coalitions occasionally, but only with impermanent victories. In 2002, opposition leaders backed the National Rainbow Coalition (NARC) and agreed to put forward a common list of candidates in the election. The NARC won a historic election in 2002 by coordinating opposition votes and taking advantage of divisions within the ruling party KANU. However, the electoral coalition fell apart after being in office for two years due to disagreements over constitutional reform. The electoral coalition was ultimately not as cohesive as many had thought in the wake of its historic win.[48]

To place Kenya in the context of this section's arguments, deficiencies in the breadth and depth of its opposition coalition could be traced back to the absence of a broad-based social movement. Given the pluralistic and divided nature of Kenyan society and the ways in which political parties are organized – bearing much resemblance to Malaysia – the pertinence of a broad-based social movement that could cross-mobilize distinct ethnic blocs and unite opposition elites cannot be underestimated. The opposition parties might be able to score a victory by cobbling together a coalition, but the coalition's lack of cohesiveness meant the victory was impermanent.

As a contrast to Kenya, let's turn to Zimbabwe. Even though Zimbabwean society is not as pluralistic or divided as Kenya or Malaysia, it serves to illustrate the general thrust of the argument that a movement-rooted opposition coalition has greater mobilizing capacity in society. The opposition alliance in

---

[48] For earlier studies on the NARC, see Howard & Roessler (2006).

Zimbabwe, the Movement for Democratic Change (MDC), is stronger than the FORD in Kenya, because of its roots in a social movement that extends into trade unions and other civil society organizations. When the labor unions in Zimbabwe evolved into an opposition party, the party members shared common values with movement supporters. Thus, social contention in Zimbabwe generally consisted of coordinated protests with clear-cut demands, which signaled the rallying capacity of the opposition parties.

In Zimbabwe, the social movement led by organized labor forged informal links between trade unions, civil society organizations, and the urban poor. The movement was subsequently transformed into a cohesive political base for the opposition MDC. This meant that by the time the MDC was launched, disparate civil society actors were no longer strangers; they had met, spoken at public meetings, organized demonstrations together, and rallied their constituents to support each other's causes (LeBas, 2011; McAdam & Tarrow, 2010).[49]

The Zimbabwe Congress of Trade Unions (ZCTU) organized and coordinated protests in the 1990s against economic hardship, which allowed it to reach into a mass constituency of urban residents, beyond the unions' formal membership. Alliance building across different civil society groups saw the formation of ZimRights, a human rights organization with membership throughout urban and rural communities, headed by the ZCTU chief, Morgan Tsvangirai (Dorman, 2001, pp. 145–149). The ZCTU emerged to be a vocal critic of the ruling party ZANU-PF, but placed an emphasis on forging "common positions, perceptions, and understandings" with other civil society organizations (LeBas, 2011, Chapter 5).

The National Constitutional Assembly (NCA), which consists of a coalition of over forty NGOs, and which is premised on pushing for constitutional reform, was formed in 1998. Much like electoral reform in Malaysia, many in Zimbabwe saw constitutionalism as a "neutral issue that could serve larger purposes," namely as "a rallying point for civil society" (Mutasah, 2001, p. 22). The NCA operated as a platform uniting a range of civil society organizations, including those with the overt aim of regime change, and others that collaborated with the government. It won a referendum on the constitution in 2000, and was seen as a viable threat to the ZANU-PF.

The mass constituency for the ZCTU and the NCA evolved into the roots of the opposition alliance, the MDC. The three organizations were run by same individuals and drew on the same support bases. The MDC utilized the organizational resources of the ZCTU to recruit members, and the NCA's networks of

---

[49] This was despite the fact that most civil society organizations maintained a degree of loyalty to the ruling party, ZANU-PF, or tried to stay away from active advocacy (Kuperus, 1999; Maxwell, 1995; Moyo, 1991; Dorman, 2002).

residents' associations to roll out political campaigns nationwide (LeBas, 2011, Chapter 7). The movements were able to channel a range of societal discontent, from economic grievances to political demands, into large-scale sustained collective actions. The opposition alliance thus benefitted from the labor movement and the constitutional movement that preceded it.

In the first parliamentary election after its establishment, the MDC won 47 percent of the popular vote, and captured 57 out of 120 seats in 2000. This marked a significant shift from the fragmentation of opposition votes that characterized the previous elections. Even though it has not yet clinched any electoral victory, in no small part due to the ruling party's vote rigging, the opposition party's high degree of cohesion was unprecedented in Zimbabwe, and rare in the African political landscape (LeBas, 2011, Chapter 7). Before the 2008 election, the MDC split into two, and the Tsvangirai-led faction forged an agreement with the ZANU-PF that saw him appointed as the prime minister. Though criticized as betraying the party's principles, the agreement was part of Tsvangirai's strategy to gain experience in order to boost the party's credibility to govern (LeBas, 2011, p. 211).

Framed in the context of this section's arguments, Zimbabwe had a broad-based movement that led to an opposition coalition that garnered widespread grassroots support. However, falling short on governing experience, the coalition has yet to establish the credibility necessary to defeat the incumbents at the ballot box.

3.5 Conclusion

Using process tracing, this section inductively builds a theory to explain how a broad-based social movement helps to bring about regime change. While the general arguments apply to all competitive authoritarian regimes, in countries where oppositions face a high bar in defeating the incumbents – because communal politics organizes society, political parties, and explains voting patterns – a broad-based nonviolent movement, a political opportunity that increases anti-regime support and facilitates elite defection, and a credible and cohesive opposition coalition are all necessary conditions for the outcome of regime change.

By bridging street politics and electoral politics, this section speaks to important existing theories on nonviolent resistance, opposition coalitions, and the ways contentious politics affect elite institutional pacts and influence regime outcomes. It corrects the postelection bias in existing movement–election literature in authoritarian contexts by putting forward the case that preelection interactions between street politics and opposition formation can similarly precipitate regime change.

Despite the lack of democratic consolidation in Malaysia, the lesson for how to build a multiparty opposition coalition from a broad-based social movement should not be lost. It took twenty years for the opposition and civil society to build trust and partnerships, and to organize half a million-strong rallies to showcase their strength and the support they enjoyed both domestically and internationally with the diasporic community. A broad-based social movement absorbed antiregime forces of all stripes, and served as a mobilizing structure to rally dissenting voices at the elite and popular levels. With the added momentum of a political opportunity, opposition parties finally came together to form a credible coalition – one that boasted a track record of governing experience – that defeated the incumbents. Credibility was key to winning the people's trust and votes. But lack of cohesiveness meant that the coalition was not glued together by common principles, and even if it could come together to compete under the same banner, it fell apart when a few elites decided to revert to the old style of authoritarian governance. Even though regime change in Malaysia proved to be fleeting, the contribution of the Bersih movement to the formation of a credible multiparty opposition coalition still offers important lessons for democratic activists around the world.

Taken together, this short monograph accentuates the pertinence of studying the interactions between street and institutional politics, and how they combine to shape regime outcomes in various manners. It contributes to important literatures in democratization and social movements in two ways. First, it proposes a new causal mechanism (a broad-based movement) that connects contentious politics with elite institutions, and explains regime-changing outcomes. Second, it recasts social movements as an independent – rather than the traditional dependent – variable that explains institutional outcomes of elite coalitions and regime change. The latter contribution, which draws evidence from the post-stolen-election movements in Eastern Europe as well as the preelection broad-based movement in Malaysia, urges scholars to revise how we traditionally view, conceptualize, and study social movements.

Interviews Conducted

1. Shahrul Aman, the interim leader of Bersih (2018), in July 2018, at Bersih headquarters, Petaling Jaya.
2. Maria Chin-Abdullah, the leader of Bersih 5.0, currently a member of the National Parliament, in July 2018, Kuala Lumpur.
3. James Chin, a Malaysian political scientist based at the University of Tasmania, November 2018, over Skype call.

4. A key opposition leader who led Bersih 1.0, July 2018, Kuala Lumpur; and November 2019, over Skype call.

5. A key civil society leader of Bersih 2.0, in July 2018, Kuala Lumpur.

6. Steven Gan, editor-in-chief, *Malaysiakini*, in July 2018, Kuala Lumpur.

7. Hew Wai Weng, a Malaysia political scientist based at the University Kebangsaan Malaysia, July 2018, Kuala Lumpur.

8. Eric Paulsen, former executive director of the NGO, Lawyers for Liberty, in July 2018, Kuala Lumpur.

9. Ho Lee Ping, an editor with a national Chinese newspaper, in July 2018, Kuching.

10. A politics lecturer at Unimas, in July 2018, Kuching.

References

Alibeyoglu, A. (2012, April 28). Police Violence Marks Malaysia Reform Rally. *Al Jazeera*. www.aljazeera.com/news/2012/4/28/police-violence-marks-malaysia-reform-rally

Anderson, D. (2005). "Yours in Struggle for Majimbo." Nationalism and the Party Politics of Decolonization in Kenya, 1955–64. *Journal of Contemporary History*, *40*(3), 547–564.

Ang, H. (2012, May 7). Bersih 3.0 violence marks a turning point. *Free Malaysia Today*. www.freemalaysiatoday.com/category/opinion/2012/05/07/bersih-3-0-violence-marks-a-turning-point

Arriola, L. R. (2012). *Multi-ethnic Coalitions in Africa: Business Financing of Opposition Election Campaigns*. Cambridge University Press.

Au, E. (2016, March 1). Mahathir Quits Umno, Calling It "Najib's Party." *The Straits Times*. www.straitstimes.com/asia/se-asia/mahathir-quits-umno-calling-it-najibs-party

BBC News. (2018, June 27). Malaysia 1MDB: Seized Tiaras, Cash and Hermes Bags "Worth $273m." BBC News. www.bbc.com/news/world-asia-44625007

Beach, D., & Pedersen, R. B. (2015). *Process-tracing Methods: Foundations and Guidelines*. University of Michigan Press.

Beissinger, M. R. (2002). *Nationalist Mobilization and the Collapse of the Soviet State*. Cambridge University Press.

Beissinger, M. R. (2007). Structure and Example in Modular Political Phenomena: The Diffusion of the Bulldozer/Rose/Orange/Tulip Revolutions. *Perspectives on Politics*, *5*(2), 259–276.

Beissinger, M. R. (2013). The Semblance of Democratic Revolution: Coalitions in Ukraine's Orange Revolution. *The American Political Science Review*, *17*(3), 574–592.

Bermeo, N. (1997). Myths of Moderation: Confrontation and Conflict During Democratic Transition. *Comparative Politics*, *29*(3), 305–322.

Binnendijk, A. L., & Marovic, I. (2006). Power and Persuasion: Nonviolent Strategies to Influence State Security Forces in Serbia (2000) and Ukraine (2004). *Communist and Post-communist Studies*, *39*(3), 411–429.

Blaydes, L. (2010). Electoral Budget Cycles and Economic Opportunism. In *Elections and Distributive Politics in Mubarak's Egypt* (pp. 77–99). Cambridge University Press.

Boix, C., & Svolik, M. (2007). The Foundations of Limited Authoritarian Government: Institutions and Power-Sharing in Dictatorships. (Unpublished manuscript.)

Boudreau, V. (2004). *Resisting Dictatorship: Repression and Protest in Southeast Asia.* Cambridge University Press.

Brancati, D. (2016). *Democracy Protests: Origins, Features, and Significance.* Cambridge University Press.

Branch, D. (2006). Loyalists, Mau Mau, and Elections in Kenya: The First Triumph of the System, 1957–1958. *Africa Today, 53*(2), 27–50.

Branch, D., & Cheeseman, N. (2006). The Politics of Control in Kenya: Understanding the Bureaucratic-executive State, 1952–78. *Review of African Political Economy, 33*(107), 11–31.

Bratton, M., & van de Walle, N. (1997). *Democratic Experiments in Africa: Regime Transitions in Comparative Perspective.* Cambridge University Press.

Brownlee, J. (2007). *Authoritarianism in an Age of Democratization.* Cambridge University Press.

Bunce, V. (1999). *Subversive Institutions: The Design and Destruction of Socialism and the State.* Cambridge University Press.

Bunce, V., & Wolchik, S. L. (2010). Defeating Dictators: Electoral Change and Stability in Competitive Authoritarian Regimes. *World Politics, 62*(1), 43–86.

Bunce, V., & Wolchik, S. L. (2011). *Defeating Authoritarian Leaders in Postcommunist Countries.* Cambridge University Press.

Bunce, V., & Wolchik, S. L. (2012). 1989 and Its Aftermath. In N. Bandelj & D. Solinger (eds.), *Socialism Vanquished, Socialism Challenged: Eastern Europe and China, 1989–2009* (pp. 23–60). Oxford University Press.

Case, B. (2020). When Yelling Isn't Good Enough: Riots and Non-violent Civil Resistance. Doctoral dissertation, University of Pittsburgh.

Cheeseman, N. (2006). Introduction: Political Linkage and Political Space in the Era of Decolonization. *Africa Today, 53*(2), 2–24.

Chenoweth, E., & Stephan, M. (2011). *Why Civil Resistance Works: The Strategic Logic of Nonviolent Conflict.* Columbia University Press.

Chin, J. (2001). Malaysian Chinese Politics in the 21st Century: Fear, Service and Marginalisation. *Asian Journal of Political Science, 9*(2), 78–94.

Chin, J., & Wong, C. H. (2009). Malaysia's Electoral Upheaval. *Journal of Democracy, 20*(3), 71–85.

Collier, R. B. (1999). *Paths Toward Democracy: The Working Class and Elites in Western Europe and South America.* Cambridge University Press.

Collins, K. (2002). Clans, Pacts, and Politics in Central Asia. *Journal of Democracy, 13*(3), 137–152.

Crouch, H. (1996). *Government and Society in Malaysia.* Cornell University Press.

Dalton, R. J., & Kuechler, M. (1990). *Challenging the Political Order: New Social and Political Movements in Western Democracies*. Oxford University Press.

della Porta, D. (2014). *Mobilizing For Democracy: Comparing 1989 and 2011*. Oxford University Press.

Diamond, L. (1999). *Developing Democracy: Toward Consolidation*. Johns Hopkins University Press.

Diamond, L. (2002). Thinking About Hybrid Regimes. *Journal of Democracy*, *13*(2), 21–35.

Diani, M., & Bison, I. (2004). Organizations, Coalitions, and Movements. *Theory and Society, 33*, 281–309.

Donno, D. (2013). Elections and Democratization in Authoritarian Regimes. *American Journal of Political Science, 57*(3), 703–716.

Dorman, S. R. (2001). Inclusion and Exclusion: NGOs and Politics in Zimbabwe. D.Phil. thesis, University of Oxford.

Dorman, S. R. (2002). "Rocking the Boat?" Church-NGOs and Democratization in Zimbabwe. *African Affairs, 101*(402), 75–92.

Earl, J. (2011). Political Repression: Iron Fists, Velvet Gloves, and Diffuse Control. *Annual Review of Sociology, 37*, 261–284.

FMT Reporters. (2016a, November 16). It's Official, Dr Mahathir Now a Bersih Man. *Free Malaysia Today*. www.freemalaysiatoday.com/category/nation/2016/11/16/its-official-dr-mahathir-now-a-bersih-man

FMT Reporters. (2016b, November 18). Police Arrest Maria Chin After Bersih Raid. *Free Malaysia Today*. www.freemalaysiatoday.com/category/nation/2016/11/18/police-arrests-maria-chin-after-bersih-raid

Franklin, J. (2019). Protest Waves and Authoritarian Regimes: Repression and Protest Outcomes. In J. Hank (ed.), *Social Movements, Nonviolent Resistance, and the State* (1st edition, pp. 98–124). Routledge.

Funston, J. (2000). Malaysia's Tenth Elections: Status Quo, "Reformasi" or Islamization? *Contemporary Southeast Asia: A Journal of International and Strategic Affairs, 22*(1), 23–59.

Gandhi, J., & Ong, E. (2019). Committed or Conditional Democrats? Opposition Dynamics in Electoral Autocracies. American Journal of Political Science, 63 (4), 948–963.

Gandhi, J., & Reuter, O. J. (2013). The Incentives for Pre-electoral Coalitions in Non-democratic Elections. *Democratization, 20*(1), 137–159.

Geddes, B. (1999). What Do We Know About Democratization After Twenty Years? *Annual Review of Political Science, 2*, 115–144.

George, A. L., & Bennett, A. (2005). Chapter 7: Case Study and the Philosophy of Science. In *Case Studies and Theory Development in the Social Sciences* (pp. 169–193). MIT Press.

Giersdorf, S., & Croissant, A. (2011). Civil Society and Competitive Authoritarianism in Malaysia. *Journal of Civil Society*, *7*(1), 1–21.

Golder, S. N. (2005). Pre-electoral Coalitions in Comparative Perspective: A Test of Existing Hypotheses. *Electoral Studies*, *24*, 643–663.

Golder, S. N. (2006). Pre-electoral Coalition Formation in Parliamentary Democracies. *British Journal of Political Science*, *36*(2), 193–212.

Goldstone, J. A. (2001). Toward a Fourth Generation of Revolutionary Theory. *Annual Review of Political Science*, *4*, 138–187.

Goldstone, J. A. (2003). *States, Parties, and Social Movements*. Cambridge University Press.

Gomez, E. T. (1991). *Money Politics in the Barisan Nasional*. Forum.

Gomez, E. T., & Jomo, K. S. (1997). *Malaysia's Political Economy: Politics, Patronage and Profits*. Cambridge University Press.

Gomez, J. (2013, September 11). GE14: 500,000 Malaysian Voters in Singapore to Generate Friction. *The Malaysia Insider*. www.themalaysianinsider.com /sideviews/article/ge14-500000-malaysian-voters-in-singapore-to-generate-friction-james-gomez (Accessed January 15, 2020.)

Haggard, S., & Kaufman, R. R. (2012). Inequality and Regime Change: Democratic Transitions and the Stability of Democratic Rule. *American Political Science Review*, *106*, 495–516.

Haggard, S., & Kaufman, R. R. (2016a). *Dictators and Democrats: Masses, Elites, and Regime Change*. Princeton University Press.

Haggard, S., & Kaufman, R. R. (2016b). Democratization During the Third Wave. *Annual Review of Political Science*, *19*, 125–144.

Hale, H. (2006). Democracy or Autocracy on the March? The Color Revolutions as Normal Dynamics of Patronal Presidentialism. *Communist and Post-communist Studies*, *39*(3), 305–329.

Harun, H. N. (2016, December 13). PPBM Officially Signs Agreement to Join Pakatan Harapan. *New Straits Times*. www.nst.com.my/news/2016/12/ 196556/ppbm-officially-signs-agreement-join-pakatan-harapan

Haynes, S. (2018, November 30). "It's About Right and Wrong." In Conversation with the Journalist Who Exposed the World's Biggest Corruption Scandal. *Time*. https://time.com/5463070/malaysia-1mdb-clare-rewcastle-brown-sarawak-report-interview

Head, J. (2020, March 5). How Malaysia's Government Collapsed in Two Years. BBC News. www.bbc.com/news/world-asia-51716474

Heaney, M. T., & Rojas, F. (2007). Partisans, Nonpartisans, and the Antiwar Movements in the United States. *American Politics Research*, *35*(4), 431–464.

Heaney, M. T., & Rojas, F. (2015). *Party in the Street: The Antiwar Movement and the Democratic Party After 9/11*. Cambridge University Press.

Hew, W. W. (2016, November 24). Bersih 5 and the increase of the Malay discontents. *New Mandala*. www.newmandala.org/bersih-5-increase-malay-discontents

Hicken, A. (2011). Clientelism. *Annual Review of Political Science, 14*, 289–310.

Higley, J., & Gunther, R. (eds.). (1992). *Elites and Democratic Consolidation in Latin America and Southern Europe*. Cambridge University Press.

Hope, B., & Wright, T. (2018). *Billion Dollar Whale: The Man Who Fooled Wall Street, Hollywood, and the World*. Hachette Books.

Howard, M., & Roessler, P. (2006). Liberalizing Electoral Outcomes in Competitive Authoritarian Regimes. *American Journal of Political Science, 50*(2), 365–381.

Hutchcroft, P. D. (1991). Oligarchs and Cronies in the Philippine State: The Politics of Patrimonial Plunder. *World Politics, 43*(3), 414–450.

Jasper, J. (1997). *The Art of Moral Protest: Culture, Biography, and Creativity in Social Movements*. University of Chicago Press.

Jomo, K. S. (2011). The New Economic Policy and Interethnic Relations in Malaysia. In *Global Minority Rights*, 239–266. Routledge.

Jones, D. M. (2000). What Mahatir Has Wrought. *The National Interest, 59*, 101–112.

Karatnycky, A., & Ackerman, P. (2005). How Freedom Is Won: From Civic Resistance to Durable Democracy. Freedom House. (Research Study.) https://freedomhouse.org/sites/default/files/How%20Freedom%20is%20Won.pdf

Karl, T. L. (1990). Dilemmas of Democratization in Latin America. *Comparative Politics, 23*(1), 1–21.

Kaufman, R. K. (1986). Liberalization and Democratization in South America: Perspectives from the 1970s. In G. O'Donnell, P. C. Schmitter, & L. Whitehead (eds.), *Transitions from Authoritarian Rule: Comparative Perspectives* (pp. 85–107). Johns Hopkins University Press.

Khoo, B. T. (2018). Borne By Dissent, Tormented by Divides: The Opposition 60 Years After Merdeka. *Southeast Asian Studies, 7*(3), 471–491.

Khoo, Y. H. (2014a). Electoral Reform Movement in Malaysia: Emergence, Protest and Reform. *Suvannabhumi: Multi-disciplinary Journal of Southeast Asian Studies, 6*(2), 81–101.

Khoo, Y. H. (2014b). Mobilization Potential and Democratization Processes of the Coalition for Clean and Fair Elections (Bersih) in Malaysia: An Interview with Hishamuddin Rais. *Austrian Journal of South-east Asian Studies, 7*(1), 111–119.

Khoo, Y. H. (2016a, November 18). Malaysia's Bersih 5 Rally: Protesters Weigh the Cost of Action Under a Repressive Regime. *The Conversation*.

https://theconversation.com/malaysias-bersih-5-rally-protesters-weigh-the-cost-of-action-under-a-repressive-regime-68723

Khoo, Y. H. (2016b). Malaysia's 13th General Elections and the Rise of Electoral Reform Movement. *Asian Politics and Policy*, *8*(3), 418–435.

Kitschelt, H. (1989). *The Logics of Party Formation: Economical Politics in Belgium and West Germany*. Cornell University Press.

Kitschelt, H., & Hellemans, S. (1990). *Beyond the European Left: Ideology and Political Action in the Belgian Ecology*. Duke University Press.

Kriesi, H., Koopmans, R., & Duyvendak, J. W. (1995). *New Social Movements in Western Europe: A Comparative Analysis*. University of Minnesota Press.

Kubik, J. (1998). Institutionalization of Protest During Democratic Consolidations in Central Europe. In D. S. Meyer and S. Tarrow (eds.) *The Social Movement Society: Contentious Politics for a New Century* (pp. 131–152). Rowman & Littlefield.

Kumar, K. (2015, August 29). Dr M Shows Up at Bersih 4 Rally, with Dr Siti Hasmah. *The Malay Mail*. www.malaymail.com/news/malaysia/2015/08/29/dr-m-shows-up-at-bersih-4-rally/960609

Kuntz, P., & Thompson, M. R. (2009). More Than Just the Final Straw: Stolen Elections as Revolutionary Triggers. *Comparative Politics*, *41*(3), 253–272.

Kuperus, T. (1999). Building Democracy: An Examination of Religious Associations in South Africa and Zimbabwe. *Journal of Modern African Studies*, *37*(4), 643–668.

Kuran, T. (1991). Now Out of Never: The Element of Surprise in the East European Revolution of 1989. *World Politics*, *44*(1), 7–48.

LeBas, A. (2011). *From Protest to Parties: Party-building and Democratization in Africa*. Oxford University Press.

Lee, J. C. H. (2007). Barisan Nasional Political Dominance and the General Elections of 2004 in Malaysia. *Sudostasian Aktuell – Journal of Current Southeast Asian Affairs*, *2*, 39–66.

Lee, J. C. H. (2014). Jom Bersih! Global Bersih and the Enactment of Malaysian Citizenship in Melbourne. *Citizenship Studies*, *18*(8), 900–913.

Levitsky, S. & Way, L. (2002). The Rise of Competitive Authoritarianism. *Journal of Democracy*, *13*(2), 51–65.

Levitsky, S., & Way, L. A. (2006). Linkage versus Leverage: Rethinking the International Dimension of Regime Change. *Comparative Politics*, *38*(4), 379–400.

Liew, C. T. (2013). An Opposition's Transformation: Interview with Liew Chin Tong. In B. Welsh & J. Chin (eds.), *Awakening: The Abdullah Badawi Years in Malaysia* (pp. 294–311). SIRD.

Lin, K. J. (2013, April 30). Ink Used on Voter's Index Finger Is NOT Indelible. *Malaysiakini*. www.malaysiakini.com/news/228547

Linz, J. J., & Stepan, A. (1996). *Problems of Democratic Transition and Consolidation: Southern Europe, South America, and Post-communist Europe*. Johns Hopkins University Press.

Liow, J. C. (2004). *A Brief Analysis of Malaysia's Eleventh General Election*. UNISCI.

Liow, J. C. (2009). *Piety and Politics: Islamism in Contemporary Malaysia*. Oxford University Press.

Lust-Okar, E. (2005). *Structuring Conflict in the Arab World: Incumbents, Opponents, and Institutions*. Cambridge University Press.

Lust-Okar, E. (2006). Elections Under Authoritarianism: Preliminary Lessons from Jordan. *Democratization, 13*(3), 455–470.

Lyn, B. S., & Ding, E. (2013, May 9). Thousands Pack Kelana Jaya Stadium for Pakatan Rally. The Malaysian Insider. https://themalaysianinsider .wordpress.com/2013/05/08/thousands-pack-kelana-jaya-stadium-for-pakata

Magaloni, B. (2006). *Voting for Autocracy: Hegemonic Party Survival and Its Demise in Mexico*. Cambridge University Press.

Mahavera, S. (2015, October 23). Is 1Malaysia Store Really Value for Money for the Working Class? The Edge Markets. www.theedgemarkets.com/art icle/1malaysia-store-really-value-money-working-class

Malaysiakini. (2015, July 29). Mammoth Bersih 4.0 Rallies to Get Najib Out. *Malaysiakini*. www.malaysiakini.com/news/306575

Malesky, E. (2009). Gerrymandering Vietnam Style: Escaping the Partial Reform Equilibrium in a Non-democratic Regime. *Journal of Politics, 71*(1), 132–159.

Marples, D. R. (2006). The Presidential Election Campaign: An Analysis. In J. Forbrig, P. Demeš, & D. R. Marples (eds.), *Prospects for Democracy in Belarus* (pp. 95–102). German Marshall Fund of the United States and the Heinrich Böll Stiftung.

Maxwell, D. (1995). The Church and Democratisation in Africa: The Case of Zimbabwe. In P. Gifford (ed.), *The Christian Churches and the Democratisation of Africa*. E. J. Brill.

McAdam, D. (1982). *Political Process and the Development of Black Insurgency, 1930–1970*. University of Chicago Press.

McAdam, D., & Kloos, K. (2014). *Deeply Divided: Racial Politics and Social Movements in Post-war America*. Oxford University Press.

McAdam, D., McCarthy, J. D., & Zald, M. N. (1996). *Comparative Perspectives on Social Movements: Political Opportunities, Mobilizing Structures, and Cultural Framings*. Cambridge University Press.

McAdam, D., & Tarrow, S. (2010). Ballots and Barricades: On the Reciprocal Relationship Between Elections and Social Movements. *Perspectives on Politics*, *8*(2), 529–542.

McAdam, D. & Tarrow, S. (2011). Social Movements and Elections: Toward a Broader Understanding of the Political Context of Contention. *Sociologias*, *13*(28), 18–51.

McAdam, D., Tarrow, S., & Tilly, C. (2001). *Dynamics of Contention*. Cambridge University Press.

McFaul, M. (2005). Transitions from Postcommunism. *Journal of Democracy*, *16*(3), 5–19.

Meladze, G. (2005, September 6). Civil Society: A Second Chance for Post-Soviet Democracy: A Eurasianet Commentary. Eurasianet. www .eurasianet.org/departments/civilsociety/articles/ eav090605.shtml

Mendoza, A. (2009). People Power in the Philippines, 1983–86. In A. Roberts & T. Garton (eds.), *Civil Resistance and Power Politics: The Experience of Non-violent Action from Gandhi to the Present* (pp. 179–182). Oxford University Press.

Meyer, D. S. (2004). Protests and Political Opportunities. *Annual Review of Sociology*, *30*, 125–145.

Meyer, D. S., & Staggenborg, S. (1996). Movements, Countermovements, and the Structure of Political Opportunity. *American Journal of Sociology*, *101* (6), 1628–1660.

Meyer, D. S., & Tarrow, S. (1998). A Movement Society: Contentious Politics for a New Century. In D. S. Meyer & S. Tarrow (eds.), *The Social Movement Society: Contentious Politics for a New Century*. Rowman & Littlefield.

Meyer, D. S., & Tarrow, S. (2018). *The Resistance: The Dawn of the Anti-Trump Opposition Movement*. Oxford University Press.

Morgenbesser, L., & Pepinsky, T. (2019). Elections as Causes of Democratization: Southeast Asia in Comparative Perspective. *Comparative Political Studies*, *52*(1), 3–35.

Moyo, S. (1991). NGO Advocacy in Zimbabwe: Systematising an Old Function or Inventing a New Role? (Working Paper No. 1. Harare.) Zimbabwe Environmental Regional Organisation.

Mueller, S. (2008). The Political Economy of Kenya's Crisis. *Journal of Eastern African Studies*, *2*(2), 185–210.

Mutasah, T. (2001). The Founding of the National Constitutional Assembly in Zimbabwe: Why, How, and Where? Unpublished manuscript, cited in LeBas (2011).

Nepstad, S. E. (2011). *Nonviolent Revolutions: Civil Resistance in the Late 20th Century*. Oxford University Press.

Noor, F. A. (1999). Looking for Reformasi: The Discursive Dynamics of the Reformasi Movement and Its Prospects as a Political Project. *Indonesia and the Malay World, 27*(77), 5–18.

Noor, F. A. (2014). *The Malaysian Islamic Party 1951–2013: Islamism in a Mottled Nation*. Amsterdam University Press.

NST Online. (2016, November 18). Bersih Rally to Go on, with or without Maria Chin. *The New Straits Times*. www.nst.com.my/news/2016/11/ 189909/bersih-rally-go-or-without-maria-chin

O'Donnell, G., Schmitter, P., & Whitehead, L. (1986). *Transitions from Authoritarian Rule: Tentative Conclusions About Uncertain Democracies*. Johns Hopkins University Press.

Ooi, K. B. (2012, November 26). The Resurgence of Social Activism in Malaysia. *ISEAS Perspective*. ISEAS.

Orvis, S. (2006). Bringing Institutions Back into the Study of Kenya and Africa. *Africa Today, 53*(2), 95–110.

Ostwald, K. (2013). How to Win a Lost Election: Malapportionment and Malaysia's 2013 General Election. *The Round Table, 102*(6), 521–532.

Paddock, R. C. (2020, July 28). Democracy Fades in Malaysia as Old Order Returns to Power. *The New York Times*. www.nytimes.com/2020/05/22/ world/asia/malaysia-politics-najib.html

Pepinsky, T. B. (2007). Autocracy, Elections and Fiscal Policy: Evidence from Malaysia. *Studies in Comparative International Development, 42*(1), 136–163.

Pepinsky, T. B. (2013). The New Media and Malaysian Politics in Historical Perspective. *Contemporary Southeast Asia, 35*(1), 83–103.

Pepinsky, T. B. (2014). The Institutional Turn in Comparative Authoritarianism. *British Journal of Political Science, 44*(3), 631–653.

Rahman, S. (2018). The Islamist Factor in Malaysia's Fourteenth General Election. *The Round Table, 107*, 669–682.

Ramesh, R. (2016, July 28). 1MDB: The Inside Story of the World's Biggest Financial Scandal. *The Guardian*. www.theguardian.com/world/2016/jul/28/ 1mdb-inside-story-worlds-biggest-financial-scandal-malaysia

Roberts, A., Mahadevan, T. K., & Sharp, G. (1967). *Civilian Defense: An Introduction*. Gandhi Peace Foundation.

Romulo, B. D. (1987). *Inside the Palace: The Rise and Fall of Ferdinand and Imelda Marcos*. G. P. Putnam's Sons.

Roundup, K. (2020, February 27). Mahathir Breaks Silence on "Sheraton Move," and 9 News from Yesterday. *Malaysiakini*. www.malaysiakini.com /news/512359

Rueschemeyer, D., Huber, E., & Stephens, J. D. (1992). *Capitalist Development and Democracy*. University of Chicago Press.

Schedler, A. (1998). What Is Democratic Consolidation? *Journal of Democracy, 9*(2), 91–107.

Schedler, A. (2013). *The Politics of Uncertainty: Sustaining and Subverting Electoral Authoritarianism*. Oxford University Press.

Schlozman, D. (2015). *When Movements Anchor Parties: Electoral Alignments in American History*. Princeton University Press.

Schock, K. (2005). *Unarmed Insurrections: People Power Movements in Nondemocracies*. University of Minnesota Press.

Schock, K. (2015). *Civil Resistance: Comparative Perspectives on Nonviolent Struggle*. University of Minnesota Press.

SD Reporters. (2015, August 29). Bersih 4: Tun M Makes Surprise Appearance. *The Sun Daily*. www.thesundaily.my/archive/1535663-CSARCH326437

Searle, P. (1999). *The Riddle of Malaysian Capitalism: Rent-seekers or Real Capitalists?* University of Hawai'i Press.

Sharp, G. (1973). *The Politics of Nonviolent Action* (Vols. 1–3). Porter Sargent.

Silitski, V. (2006). Belarus: Learning from Defeat. *Journal of Democracy, 17* (4), 138–152.

Simpser, A. (2005). Making Votes Not Count: Strategic Incentives for Electoral Corruption. PhD thesis, Stanford University.

Skocpol, T., & Williamson, V. (2016). *The Tea Party and the Remaking of Republican Conservatism*. Oxford University Press.

Slater, D. (2003). Iron Cage in an Iron Fist: Authoritarian Institutions and the Personalization of Power in Malaysia. *Comparative Politics, 36*(1), 81–101.

Slater, D. (2010). *Ordering Power: Contentious Politics and Authoritarian Leviathans in Southeast Asia*. Cambridge University Press.

Slater, D. (2012). Strong-state Democratization in Malaysia and Singapore. *Journal of Democracy, 23*(2), 19–33.

Subramaniam, P. (2014, March 7). Anwar Given 5 Years' Jail After Appellate Court Reverses Sodomy Acquittal. *The Malay Mail*. www.malaymail.com /news/malaysia/2014/03/07/anwar-acquittal-reversed/630827

Svolik, M. W. (2019). Polarization versus Democracy. *Journal of Democracy, 30*(3), 20–32.

Tarrow, S. G. (1989). *Democracy and Disorder: Protest and Politics in Italy, 1965–1975*. Oxford University Press.

Tarrow, S. G. (1998). *Power in Movement: Social Movements and Contentious Politics* (2nd edition). Cambridge University Press.

Tarrow, S. G. (2021). *Movements and Parties: Critical Connections in American Political Development*. Cambridge University Press.

The Irish Times. (1998, September 29). Violence Erupts as Protest Movement Takes to Streets Against Malaysia MP. *The Irish Times*.

The Star. (2015, August 27). Police Probe Anti-Bersih "Red Shirts" After Self-defence Skills. *The Star*. www.thestar.com.my/News/Nation/2015/08/27/bersih-4-police-to-probe-red-shirts

The Straits Times. (2016, November 16). Mahathir Appears in Bersih 5 T-shirt in New Video, Calls on Malaysians to Join Rally. *The Straits Times*. www.straitstimes.com/asia/se-asia/mahathir-appears-in-bersih-5-t-shirt-in-new-video-calls-on-malaysians-to-join-rally

The World Bank. (2011). Malaysia Economic Monitor: Brain Drain. http://documents.worldbank.org/curated/en/282391468050059744/pdf/614830WP0malay10Box358348B01PUBLIC1.pdf

The World Bank. (2017). GDP per Capita (current US$). https://data.worldbank.org/indicator/NY.GDP.PCAP.CD

Thompson, M. R. (1995). *The Anti-Marcos Struggle: Personalistic Rule and Democratic Transition in the Philippines*. Yale University Press.

Thompson, M. R. (1996). Off the Endangered List: Philippine Democratization in Comparative Perspective. *Comparative Politics*, *28*(2), 197–205.

Tilly, C. (1978). *From Mobilization to Revolution*. Addison-Wesley.

Trejo, G. (2014). The Ballot and the Street: An Electoral Theory of Social Protest in Autocracies. *Perspectives on Politics*, *12*(2), 332–352.

Tucker, J. A. (2007). Enough! Electoral Fraud, Collective Action Problems, and Post-communist Colored Revolutions. *Perspectives on Politics*, *5*(3), 535–551.

Tufekci, Z., & Wilson, C. (2012). Social Media and the Decision to Participate in Political Protest: Observations from Tahrir Square. *Journal of Communication*, *62*(2), 363–379.

Ufen, A. (2020). Opposition in Transition: Pre-electoral Coalitions and the 2018 Electoral Breakthrough in Malaysia. *Democratization*, *27*(2), 167–184. •

Ulfelder, J. (2005). Contentious Collective Action and the Breakdown of Authoritarian Regimes. *International Political Science Review*, *26*(3), 311–334.

Wahman, M. (2013). Opposition Coalitions and Democratization by Election. *Government and Opposition*, *48*(1), 3–32.

Wan Jan, W. S. (2018). *Parti Pribumi Bersatu Malaysia in Johor: New Party, Big Responsibility*. ISEAS – Yusof Ishak Institute.

Weiss, M. (1999). What Will Become of Reformasi? Ethnicity and Changing Political Norms in Malaysia. *Contemporary Southeast Asia, 21*(3), 424–450.

Weiss, M. L. (2006). *Protest and Possibilities: Civil Society and Coalitions for Political Change in Malaysia.* Stanford University Press.

Weiss, M. L. (2013). Malaysia's 13th General Elections: Same Result, Different Outcome. *Asian Survey, 53*(6), 1135–1158.

Weiss, M. L. (2016). Payoffs, Parties, or Policies: "Money Politics" and Electoral Authoritarian Resilience. *Critical Asian Studies, 48*(1), 77–99.

Wong, C. H. (2005). The Federal and State Elections in Malaysia, March 2004. *Electoral Studies, 24*(2), 311–319.

Wong, C. H. (2018, July). Interview with Chin-Huat Wong, a Bersih Leader. (Personal communication.)

Wright, T., & Clark, S. (2015, July 2). Investigators Believe Money Flowed to Malaysian Leader Najib's Accounts Amid 1MDB Probe. *The Wall Street Journal.* www.wsj.com/articles/malaysian-investigators-probe-points-to-deposits-into-prime-ministers-accounts-1435866107?tesla=y

Zahiid, S. J., & Lin, M. M. (2015, August 29). To Prove Critics Wrong, Muslims Pray at Bersih 4 Rally. *The Malay Mail.* www.malaymail.com/news/malaysia/2015/08/29/to-prove-critics-wrong-muslims-pray-at-bersih-4-rally/960435

Ziegfeld, A., & Tudor, M. (2017). How Opposition Parties Sustain Single-party Dominance: Lessons from India. *Party Politics, 23*(3), 262–273.

Zunes, S. (1999). The Origins of People Power in the Philippines. In S. Zunes, L. R. Kurtz, & S. B. Asher (eds.), *Nonviolent Social Movements: A Geographical Perspective* (pp. 129–157). Blackwell.

Acknowledgments

In 2017, I heard Sidney Tarrow speak at a convention about the interactions between movements and political parties in American politics. Donald Trump's election to the White House at that time sparked a great deal of interest in the scholarly community about what it meant for American democracy. I remember being very intrigued by the idea of analyzing social movements alongside political parties and elections. I was especially interested given the traditional division of labor between the disciplines of political science and sociology, in that the former tends to focus on institutional politics and the latter on social movements. (Of course, this is a simplification, but it largely holds true.)

A year later, in 2018, the National Front coalition government in Malaysia was voted out of office, ending its sixty-one-year rule as one of the world's most durable autocratic regimes. The interest it sparked was nowhere near the scale of Trump's presidency, but it was a major political event that engrossed scholars of authoritarianism and Southeast Asia. Malaysia is a multiethnic society ruled by a multiparty coalition, and was governed for the last six decades through a mixture of high-growth economic policies, cronyistic preferential redistribution, and low- to medium-grade state repression.

To me, the most puzzling aspect of the regime change in 2018 was its relation – or lack thereof – to the electoral movement, Bersih, that had developed for over a decade preceding the historic election. This Element builds on an earlier paper that explains Malaysia's regime change through the lens of movement rally–election interactions. The earlier paper, which became the foundation of the section on Malaysia, benefitted enormously from the generosity of colleagues from the Southeast Asian Research Group (SEAREG). Among them Allen Hicken, Tom Pepinsky, Meredith Weiss, and Dan Slater took time to discuss ideas and read my drafts (sometimes more than once!). Meredith Weiss, with her unparalleled knowledge of the social movement and political landscape in Malaysia, provided me with detailed and critical feedback. I also benefitted from the wisdom of colleagues who acted as discussants in the workshops where I presented the earlier draft paper – Tricia Yeoh, Dana Moss, Charles Crabtree, Adam Casey, and Lucan Way, among others. I would also like to thank Brodie Hemphill, Ming-han Sun, and Mary Qiu for excellent research assistance.

I want to convey enormous gratitude to the series editors, David S. Meyer and Suzanne Staggenborg, for being so enthusiastic about this project right from the beginning, and for patiently guiding and seeing it through.

I owe the utmost gratitude to my interlocutors in Malaysia and the Malaysian diasporas, who took time to share with me their personal stories, including tales of joy, frustration, and sorrow about the movement and the system. In many respects, this is a story of *hope* and *hard work* – of how, over a twenty-year period, an imagined, worldwide community of peaceful demonstrators clad in yellow T-shirts brought down a regime. While political events may be impermanent, the lessons learned will often stick with us for a long time.

As this Element goes to print, I have learned that Sidney Tarrow's *Movements and Parties* is also forthcoming at the Cambridge University Press, which will no doubt shape how scholars think about these issues in American politics and beyond. Together with his monograph, I hope this work will promote more research on the interactions between social movements and institutional politics.

Cambridge Elements

Contentious Politics

David S. Meyer
University of California, Irvine

David S. Meyer is Professor of Sociology and Political Science at the University of California, Irvine. He has written extensively on social movements and public policy, mostly in the United States, and is a winner of the John D. McCarthy Award for Lifetime Achievement in the Scholarship of Social Movements and Collective Behavior.

Suzanne Staggenborg
University of Pittsburgh

Suzanne Staggenborg is Professor of Sociology at the University of Pittsburgh. She has studied organizational and political dynamics in a variety of social movements, including the women's movement and the environmental movement, and is a winner of the John D. McCarthy Award for Lifetime Achievement in the Scholarship of Social Movements and Collective Behavior.

About the series

Cambridge Elements series in Contentious Politics provides an important opportunity to bridge research and communication about the politics of protest across disciplines and between the academy and a broader public. Our focus is on political engagement, disruption, and collective action that extends beyond the boundaries of conventional institutional politics. Social movements, revolutionary campaigns, organized reform efforts, and more or less spontaneous uprisings are the important and interesting developments that animate contemporary politics; we welcome studies and analyses that promote better understanding and dialogue.

Cambridge Elements ☰

Contentious Politics

Elements in the series

A full series listing is available at: www.cambridge.org/ECTP